The Care Homes Legal Handbook

of related interest

Law, Rights and Disability
Edited by Jeremy Cooper
ISBN 1 85302 836 3

Good Practice with Vulnerable Adults
Edited by Jacki Pritchard
ISBN 1 85302 892 3

Manual Handling in Health and Social Care
An A-Z of Law and Practice
Michael Mandelstam
ISBN 1 84310 041 X

Equipment for Older or Disabled People and the Law
Michael Mandelstam
ISBN 1 85302 352 3

Care Services for Later Life
Transformations and Critiques
Edited by Tony Warnes, Mike Nolan and Lorna Warren
ISBN 1 85302 852 5

**Including the Person with Dementia in Designing
and Delivering Care**
'I Need to Be Me!'
Elizabeth Barnett
ISBN 1 85302 740 5

Community Care Practice and the Law
Second Edition
Michael Mandelstam
ISBN 1 85302 647 6

An A-Z of Community Care Law
Michael Mandelstam
ISBN 1 85302 560 7

Advocacy Skills for Health and Social Care Professionals
Neil Bateman
ISB 1 85302 865 7

Disabled Children and the Law
Research and Good Practice
Second Edition
Janet Read, Luke Clements and David Ruebain
ISBN 1 84310 280 3

The Care Homes Legal Handbook

Jeremy Cooper

Jessica Kingsley Publishers
London and Philadelphia

First published in 2006
by Jessica Kingsley Publishers
116 Pentonville Road
London N1 9JB, UK
and
400 Market Street, Suite 400
Philadelphia, PA 19106, USA

www.jkp.com

Library of Congress Cataloging in Publication Data
A CIP catalog record for this book is available from the Library of Congress

British Library Cataloguing in Publication Data
A CIP catalogue record for this book is available from the British Library

ISBN-10: 1 84310 064 9
ISNB-13: 978 1 84310 0645

Contents

Note on Terminology

It is anticipated that many (though not all) of the users of this handbook will not be lawyers. The book is written in a style that seeks to take account of this fact. By way of an introduction therefore, I include the following note on terminology to assist those who may need further clarification.

Law

Law comes principally in the form of *statutes*, which often need to be explained and interpreted by judges through *cases*. In addition to statute law and case-law (described collectively as *primary law*), law also appears in the form of *directions, approvals* and *regulations*, often set out in *statutory instruments (SIs)* (described collectively as *secondary law*). Secondary law has the same legal force as primary law, and contains the detail necessary to operationalise primary law. It can therefore be of great significance in this field.

The full text of any statutes or statutory instruments can be found online at www.hmso.gov.uk. The service is available from 1988 for statutes, or from 1997 for statutory instruments.

The Care Standards Act 2000 constitutes the main source of primary law relating to the regulation of care homes. However, much important practical detail is contained in the secondary law of regulations, which are published as statutory instruments and directions.

Guidance

The distinction between directions and guidance is not always clear, but it is important to be able to make this distinction. In the case of *R v North Derbyshire Health Authority ex p. Fisher* (1998)[1] the Court offered the following clarification:

> If it is the intention of the Secretary of State to give Directions which attract a statutory duty of compliance, then (s)he should make it clear that this is what (s)he is doing. The difference between a policy which provides mere guidance and one which the authority is obliged to implement is critical. Policy which is in the form of guidance can be expressed in strong terms, and yet fall short of amounting to Directions.

Guidance appears in a bewildering range of formats, which can be both contradictory and confusing. It may appear in codes of practice, policy guidance, practice guidance, circulars, advice or charters. These in turn are produced from a variety of sources, primarily the Department of Health, the Department of Social Security, and the Social Services Inspectorate (which is part of the Department of Health). The basic rule is that *guidance is not law*, and is therefore intrinsically of less importance than law. These documents are however helpful as guides to interpretation, and are likely to be quoted or used in court proceedings as a means to determine whether a person has acted reasonably or appropriately in any given situation.

There is one type of guidance that *does* have more or less the force of law, namely policy guidance that is issued under s.7 of the Local Authority Social Services Act 1970 (LASSA). This is because s.7 of this Act states that 'local authorities have a duty to act under the general guidance of the Secretary of State', which effectively creates a legal duty to follow guidance of this nature. In the case of *R v Islington LBC ex p. Rixon* (1996)[2] the judge held that:

> s.7 requires local authorities to follow the path charted by the Secretary of State's guidance, with liberty to deviate from it where the local authority judges on admissible grounds that there is good reason to do so, but without freedom to take a substantially different course.

It is therefore important to be able to identify whether any particular guidance was issued as 'policy guidance' by the Secretary of State, under the provisions of LASSA (LASSA guidance). If the guidance was LASSA guidance, a local authority can only refuse to follow it in a particular case if they can give clear and adequate reasons for such deviation, to a high standard of proof. LASSA guidance is often headed LAC (Local Authority Circular) which usually, *though not necessarily*, implies that the guidance is LASSA guidance. If it is LASSA guidance it should be described as such in the preamble to the document.

An example of LASSA policy guidance is *Community Care in the Next Decade and Beyond: Policy Guidance*, issued by the DoH in 1990, and described by the judge in *R v Sutton LBC ex p. Turner* (1998)[3] as 'clearly binding on local authorities'. Finally it should be noted that the National Care Standards Commission must, in the exercise of its functions, act 'under the general guidance of the secretary of State'.[4]

The National Health Services Act 1977 s.13 empowers the Health Secretary to issue directions to NHS bodies, which will also have the force of law. But there is no specific statute concerning DoH guidance equivalent to that governing LASSA guidance. DoH guidance is therefore technically no more than 'guidance'. With the closer merging of the health and social services, however, this is likely to change.

For copies of some of the key guidance for England and Wales[5] issued since 1 January 1995, and most other DoH publications, enter the DoH website at www.doh.gov.uk and click on POINT. For copies of all circulars published since that date click on COIN. Hard copies of guidance can also be obtained free of charge from the Department of Health, PO Box 777, London SE1 6XH, fax: 01623#724524, or email doh@prologistic.co.uk. The text of many pre-1995 local authority circulars and social services letters can be found on http://www.doh.gov.uk/public/letters/lasslh.htm

ENDNOTES

1   (1998) 1 CCLR 150.
2   (1998) 1 CCLR 119.
3   (1998) 1 CCLR 251.
4   Care Standards Act s.6. For an example of such guidance see Chapter One, Note 24.
5   Note that all Welsh Assembly guidance issued since June 1999 can be found at http://www.assembly.wales.gov.uk.

The New Regulatory Framework

INTRODUCTION

A care home is:

> An establishment providing accommodation, together with nursing or personal care, for any of the following:

- persons who are, or have been, ill;
- persons who have, or have had, a mental disorder;
- persons who are disabled or infirm;
- persons who are, or have been, dependent on alcohol or drugs.

An establishment *is not* a care home unless the care which it provides includes assistance with bodily functions where such assistance is required.[1] Note that to be classified as a 'care home', it is only necessary for the home to *provide for* any of the above categories of individual. It is not necessary that *every* resident falls into one or more of the categories.

According to Tim Ward of Care Aware,[2] a good care home has the following features:

- It is well-known in the local area.
- It has a reputation for providing good care.
- It has a good mix of staff, who get on well.
- It has a low staff turnover, with minimum use of agency staff.
- It offers an effective training programme, for *all* its staff.
- It offers a nice environment, with both property and grounds well-maintained.
- It has high occupancy levels.
- It offers a reasonable percentage of privately funded beds.

- It has a marketing plan, that works.

- It offers an overall fees structure at a rate to meet costs and make a reasonable profit.

- It has a good manager.

This checklist provides an excellent summary of the key components of a successfully run care home. But in the regulated world of the twenty-first century, there is a further key dimension to the successful running of a care home, namely that all concerned have a clear understanding and appreciation of the legal regulatory framework within which care homes operate. A mass of new laws, regulations, standards, training requirements, policy documents and new organisational structures have changed the landscape of care home management irreversibly. This handbook explains to care home managers and care home staff, to care home regulators and care home inspectors, precisely what the new legal framework requires of all involved, what it is designed to achieve, and how it is designed to operate.

The number of residential care homes in the UK subject to external regulation is in excess of 30,000,[3] of which over 20,000 are in the private and voluntary sectors.[4] Prior to April 2002, the regulatory system for residential care homes was diverse, multi-layered and widely inconsistent. Responsibility for the regulation and inspection of care homes was shared between the local inspection units of 150 local and 80 health authorities, who applied local standards 'on an individual and variable basis',[5] together with local authority social services departments, who had responsibility for regulating their own homes. The system appeared inconsistent, disorganised and demoralised. In June 2000, William Laing offered a series of revealing statistics, in support of this analysis:[6]

- Care home deregistrations are on the increase: 8000 beds were deregistered in the year 2000 (2500 of these in local authority homes, the majority of the remainder in small private care homes), as against 2500 beds deregistered in 1995.

- New registrations are in decline: 500 beds in 2000, as against 4800 beds in 1995. The great majority of new registrations were in the private sector.

- Spare capacity in the residential home sector is now only 9 per cent,[7] and significantly lower in certain 'hot spot' areas, such as Cambridge and Brighton.

- Although the severe downward pressure of local authorities on the standard fee (in 2000) was starting to give way in some areas, profit margins in the most successful care homes have declined to a maximum of 25–30 per cent income, and are normally less.

- The impact of the raising of the national minimum wage, the latest nurses' pay settlement[8] and free nursing care (from autumn 2001) is likely to provoke a serious cost inflation in the sector.

- Thirty per cent of residents are now 'self-funders',[9] plus many others adding top-ups to the local authority payment. This is likely to increase with the impact of property inflation.

For a long time, the Department of Health (DoH) and local authorities have been debating the need for a change in the system, often in close discussion, though not necessarily in agreement, with the private care home sector. This period of intensive planning and legislation to achieve the plans has finally come to a close. From April 2002, the new framework designed to change the face of care home regulation forever has come into effect.

REGISTRATION AND REGULATION OF STANDARDS IN CARE HOMES: THE NEW FRAMEWORK

The Care Standards Act 2000[10] has created two new independent bodies to regulate, inspect, monitor and set standards for all agencies and establishments providing social care, including care homes, in England and in Wales. The independent body for England is called the National Care Standards Commission.[11] The independent body for Wales is called the Care Standards Inspectorate for Wales.[12] The Scottish system is governed by separate legislation, the Regulation of Care (Scotland) Act 2001, with its own independent body, the Scottish Commission for the Regulation of Care.[13]

The National Care Standards Commission has wide-ranging duties, powers and responsibilities, including registering, deregistering, inspecting and regulating the activities of all care homes. The three component parts of the regulatory framework for which the Commission has overall responsibility are:

1. The Care Standards Act 2000.

2. The Regulations (issued by the Secretary of State as statutory instruments).[14]

3. The National Minimum Standards.[15]

This book will examine each of these components in some detail.

TRANSITIONAL ARRANGEMENTS FOR NEW REGULATORY FRAMEWORK

Care homes that, on 1 April 2002, were already registered with a local council or health authority or were approved by the DoH, were automatically registered with the Commission, *subject to having completed a transfer of registration form*, before that date. The Commission intends to inspect all these automatically registered care homes, including local authority homes, in the course of 2002–3, to ensure that they comply with the relevant regulations, and that they meet the new National Minimum Standards. Local authority inspection units have closed down, with most staff transferring to the Commission. Anne Parker, the Commission Chair, has stated that in cases where there is an initial marginal failure to meet the new Standards in full, a flexible approach is likely to be adopted. This will allow the care home time to reach the standard, if the inspectors are convinced from the evidence of the home's previous record, that they are likely to deliver the standard in a reasonable time frame. She has made it clear that in the first year of its operation, the Commission will focus upon finding out how people achieve outcomes, not upon closing down homes. This view has been reinforced in Government Guidance which states its keenness to ensure that 'initially a pragmatic, but timed approach is taken with regard to compliance'.[16] Care homes seeking registration for the first time, after April 2002, will be registered only if they comply with the Regulations and meet the National Minimum Standards. Registration can be conditional or unconditional. If on 1 April 2002 a notice of improvement or other enforcement notice was in place on a care home, any follow-up/enforcement requirements will become the responsibility of the Commission.

DEFINITIONS

As stated above, a 'care home' is an establishment providing accommodation, together with nursing or personal care, for persons who are, or have been, ill; persons who have, or have had, a mental disorder; persons who are disabled or infirm; persons who are, or have been, dependent on alcohol or drugs.

Note that the provision of board (e.g. food) is no longer included in the definition of a care home, nor is there a reference to any age requirement. The word 'infirm', however, whilst not defined in the Act, is defined in the dictionary as 'a person weak in health or body, especially from old age'.[17]

'Personal care', whilst not defined in the Act, was defined by the Royal Commission on Long Term Care for the Elderly as 'care that directly involves touching a person's body, and therefore incorporates issues of intimacy, personal dignity and confidentiality and is distinct from both treatment-/therapy and from indirect care such as home-help or the provision of meals'.[18]

The word 'ill' is not defined in the Act. But it should be noted that the Secretary of State's Directions and Approvals 1993[19] have recommended that care and attention may be required, not merely because the person is ill, but in order to prevent that person becoming ill, or by way of after-care.

A disabled person does not need to demonstrate that his/her disability is 'substantial and permanent'[20] for the purposes of entering a care home.

The 'mental disorder' definition includes accommodation provided to a person in order to help prevent mental disorder, and for after-care purposes. This includes provision for those with no settled residence, who are nevertheless in the local authority's area.[21]

In contrast the alcohol or drug dependency provisions are limited to a person with dependency, and do not extend to prevention.[22]

WHAT ARE THE GENERAL DUTIES OF THE NATIONAL CARE STANDARDS COMMISSION?

The Commission must act in accordance with any directions in writing given to it by the Secretary of State and under the general guidance of the Secretary of State.[23] Any such directions will be legally binding on the Commission and must be followed. Guidance of this nature must also be followed, unless there is a compelling reason not to do so.[24] The general duties of the Commission fall into three broad categories as follows:

1. Providing information.

    The Commission has a general responsibility to keep the Secretary of State and the general public informed about the availability and the standard of provision in England, of all care homes.[25]

2. Encouraging improvement.

    The Commission has the general duty to encourage improvement in the quality of these services.[26]

3. Giving advice.

    The Commission has the duty to provide the Secretary of State with advice as follows:

    *   At any time, on any changes to the National Minimum Standards, they think necessary in order to improve the quality of care homes' services,[27] or on any matter connected with the provision of these services.[28]

- When asked to do so by the Secretary of State, on such matters
  relating to the provision of these services as the Secretary of State
  requests.[29]

Note that none of the above duties relates to the provision of medical or psy-
chiatric treatment. This is because the regulation of such services is in the
hands of a different body, the Commission for Health Improvement (CHI). [30]
There is however a general provision in the Care Standards Act permitting the
Commission and the CHI to carry out each other's functions, if authorised to
do so by Regulations.[31]

HOW IS RESPONSIBILITY FOR CARRYING OUT THESE DUTIES DELEGATED?

The National Care Standards Commission has overall responsibility for
exercising the regulatory functions associated with care homes. It has an
annual budget in excess of £100m. At full strength the Commission is
projected to employ around 2500 staff located in 80 offices across the country
(1 national office, 8 regional offices, and 71 area offices). The headquarters of
the Commission in Newcastle, employing around 100 staff, will have overall
responsibility for strategy. The area offices will deal with the day-to-day
activities of registration, inspection, the investigation of complaints and
enforcement of decisions, supported by the regional office infrastructure.

The registration and inspection officers who will have responsibility for
these tasks are all trained according to the National Occupational Standards
for Regulators of Social and Health Care for Adults and Children. The first
qualification for inspectors of health and social care was launched by the
General Social Care Council in October 2001, and came into effect in March
2002.[32] The National Occupational Standards 'describe the complex and
demanding functions of carrying out the regulations of health and social care
as provided by the Care Standards Act' and 'define good practice by describing
the competence required for specific occupational roles.'[33] These Standards set
down a series of statements of 'competence requirements', which will form the
basis of all training and qualifications in this field. The 'competence requirements' have the following general functions:

- They describe good practice in particular areas of work, bringing
  together the skills, knowledge and values necessary to do the
  work.

- They provide a benchmark against which to measure individual
  performance through self-assessment.

- They provide managers and practitioners with a tool for a wide variety of workforce management, continuous professional development and quality assurance activities.

The National Occupational Standards are accredited by the qualifications accreditation bodies in England, Wales and Scotland.[34] Anne Parker has stated her intention that the core objectives of the Commission will be to deliver consistency in an open and accountable way, to raise the profile of quality management in the sector generally, to contribute to greater synergy between the health and social care sectors, and to ensure that the outcomes set out in the Care Homes National Minimum Standards are met.[35]

TRAINING AND REGISTRATION OF INDIVIDUALS IN CARE HOMES

There are currently around 70,000 managers, deputies and supervisors working in some 30,000 adult residential and nursing homes in England alone, covering a very wide range of needs.[36] A great number of these people are in positions of complex responsibility without any formal training for the job. A system of National Occupational Standards is being introduced as the *training framework* that will lead to registration and regulations specifying the legal management training requirements.[37] Training Standard 28,[38] designed to ensure that residents are in safe hands at all times, requires that within each home:

> A minimum ratio of 50 per cent trained members of care staff (NVQ level 2 or equivalent) must be achieved by 2005, excluding the registered manager and/or care manager, and in care homes providing nursing, excluding those members of the care staff who are registered nurses.[39] Trainees, including all staff under 18, must be registered on a TOPSS-certified[40] training programme.[41]

Linked to the training framework, the Government has introduced a new system for the registration of individuals working in residential care settings, beginning with those in management and supervisory positions. Registration is under the overall control and supervision of the General Social Care Council (GSCC), which came into being in October 2001 and issued its first set of draft codes of conduct and practice for the social care workforce for consultation early in 2002. Details of the Training and Staff Registration Framework can be found in Chapter Nine. In February 2002 the Government announced the commitment of £15m ring-fenced to support staff training care[42].

ENDNOTES

1.   s.3 Care Standards Act 2000 (hereafter referred to as CSA), and s.121(a).

2.   Care Aware is an independent public information and advice service that specialises in all issues of care for older people. These remarks were made in a presentation delivered at the National Care Homes Association Annual Conference in Solihull, 13 June 2001.

3.   *National Care Standards Commission (Registration) Regulations 2001, Consultation Document: Regulatory Impact Assessment* (DoH 2001) para. 9.1.

4.   Figures taken from the *A–Z Care Homes Guide 2001,* Hungerford: Tomorrow's Guides Ltd.

5.   *National Care Standards Commission (Registration) Regulations 2001, Consultation Document: Regulatory Impact Assessment* (DoH 2001) para. 6.3.

6.   Managing Director of the consultancy firm Laing and Buisson. These remarks were made in a presentation delivered in Solihull, 13 June 2001 (see Note 2). A further detailed analysis of the costs of care, identifying a mismatch between fees paid and costs incurred, was published in 2001 by Susan Doohan of the Independent Healthcare Association, ISBN 1 89932 802 5.

7.   And, in addition, there is a 1.6 per cent net annual loss of capacity.

8.   Some 50,000 nurses are currently working in the residential care sector.

9.   This group includes those who pay some of their fees from social security benefits, such as Disability Living Allowance.

10. The full text of the Act can be found at http://www.hmso.gov.uk/acts /acts2000/20000014.htm

11. The National Care Standards Commission is an 'executive Non Departmental Public Body, which has some independence from the DoH, with an independent Chair, Chief Executive and Board. It will be set targets and be monitored by DoH Ministers' (DoH website). Based in Newcastle it will oversee a regional network, with 8 regional directors, and a total of 72 area offices dealing with day-to-day operational activities.

12. The Inspectorate operates as an operationally independent Division of the Welsh Assembly, based at eight regional locations across Wales. Whilst the primary Westminster legislation, the Care Standards Act 2000, applies in Wales, the development of any associated Regulations, Standards and Policies on such matters as Nursing Fees, has been devolved to the Welsh framework. For further information consult www.wales.gov.uk/subisocialpolicycare standards/

13. The full text of the Scottish legislation can be downloaded from the website www.hmso.gov.uk. and the website of the Scottish Commission can be visited at www.carecommission.com. The Scottish Parliament is responsible for legislating all Regulations that will operationalise the system in Scotland. The Scottish Executive has tasked their National Care Standards Committee with establishing National Minimum Standards for Care Homes. The Scottish Parliament has taken a radically different approach to the funding of care in care homes, from their English or Welsh counterparts, a matter of ongoing controversy. See Community Care andHealth (Scotland) Bill 2002.

14   The Care Homes Regulations 2001, SI 3965; The National Care Standards Commission (Registration) Regulations 2001, SI 3969; The National Care Standards Commission (Fees and Frequency of Inspections) Regulations 2001, SI 3980; The Protection of Children and Vulnerable Adults and Care Standards Tribunal Regulations, 2002.

15   The full texts of the National Minimum Standards and the Care Homes Regulations 2001 are contained in *Care Homes for Older People* (2nd Edition, 2002) DOH, available to download at www.doh.gov.uk/ncsc/carehomesfor olderpeople.pdf

16   Anne Parker was quoted in *Community Care*, 25th–31st October 2001, p.14. The Government's *Guidance on the Implementation of Regulations and National Minimum Standards* was issued under s.6 CSA on 29th Jan, 2002.

17   *Collins English Dictionary.*

18   *With Respect to Old Age: Long Term Care – Rights and Responsibilities. A Report by the Royal Commission on Long Term Care.* Cm 4192-I, March 1999, HMSO, at 6.43.

19   LAC (93) 10 Appendix 1 para. 2.5.

20   This is the definition that triggers an assessment for a range of disability related services under s.2 of the Chronically Sick and Disabled Persons Act 1970.

21   LAC (93) 10 Appendix 1 para. 2.3.

22   LAC (93) 10 Appendix 1 para. 2.6.

23   s.6(1) CSA.

24   See Note on Terminology. The first piece of guidance to be issued under this section dated 29/1/02 was *Guidance on the Implementation of Regulations and National Minimum Standards* by the NCSC.

25   s.7(1)(3) CSA.

26   s.7(2) CSA.

27   s.7(5)(a) CSA.

28   s.7(5)(b) CSA. Note that the Commission Chair, Anne Parker, has made it clear that the Commission has decided not to comment on the minimum standards set by the government, until they have gathered sufficient information on their operation in the first year of the new system (see Note 16).

29   2.7(4) CSA.

30   The CHI began work in April 2000. Its overall brief is to improve the quality of patient care in the NHS across England and Wales by undertaking a comprehensive programme of clinical governance reviews. To achieve this goal CHI will visit every NHS Trust and local authority, including primary care groups, local health groups and general practices, on a rolling programme every four years. For website go to: http://www.chi.nhs.uk/

31   s.9(1) CSA.

32   *Community Care*, 25–31 October 2001, p.15, and 28 Feb–6 March 2002, p.11. The new qualification is to be called the Regulation of Care Services Award.

33   National Occupational Standards for Regulators of Social and Health Care for Adults and Children, June 2001, p.2. See http://www.doh.gov.uk/pub/docs/doh/nosr1.pdf

34   England: Quality Curriculum Authority (QCA). Wales: Qualifications, Curriculum and Assessment Authority/Awdurdod Cymwmsterau,

Cwricwlwm ac Asesu Cymru (ACCAC). Scotland: Scottish Qualifications Authority (SCA).

35   Speaking in Solihull, 13 June 2001 (see Note 2).

36   These figures are produced by the National Care Standards Commission and by TOPSS, which is the National Training Organisation (NTO) for the Personal Social Services. NTOs are independent, employer-led sector organisations recognised by the DfES to work strategically with their sectors, and with Government, across education and training for the whole of the United Kingdom.

37   s.22(2)(h) CSA.

38   See Chapter Nine at p.125.

39   A 'registered nurse' means a nurse registered by the Nursing and Midwifery Council, with a qualification in nursing, midwifery of health visiting recognised by the Council. Any agency staff working in the home are included in the 50 per cent ratio.

40   See Note 36.

41   This issue is dealt with in more detail in Chapter Nine, pp.124–7.

42   Community Care, 21–27 Febuary 2002, p.10.

CHAPTER TWO

What are the Specific Duties of the National Care Standards Commission?

REGISTRATION

All care homes must be registered with the National Care Standards Commission, in order to operate lawfully under the Care Standards Act 2000. Any person who carries on or manages a care home without being registered in respect of it will be guilty of a criminal offence.[1] Where the activities of a care home are carried on from two or more branches, each of those branches shall be treated as a separate agency for the purposes of registration.[2]

The detail of all the procedures necessary for registration, variation or removal of any conditions of registration are contained in The National Care Standards Commission (Registration) Regulations 2001[3] (referred to hereafter in this chapter as the Registration Regulations: see Appendix). Outline inspection procedures are contained in The National Care Standards Commission (Fees and Frequency of Inspections) Regulations 2001 and 2003.[4]

What is the procedure for registration?

An organisation or a person (described as the 'responsible person') wishing to be registered must first fill out an application form seeking registration with the Commission. The application must be accompanied by a non-refundable fee, set by the Secretary of State. The application/registration fee for homes in 2002–3 is as follows:[5]

Homes with fewer than four registered places: £300

All other homes: £1100

Where a manager who is not the owner or provider also needs to be registered, an additional fee of £300 will be levied.

The previous system, whereby a home providing both residential care *and* nursing care had to obtain dual registration from the local authority inspection unit and the health authority, has been discontinued, and all aspects of registration are now covered in the single registration. In addition to initial registration fees, care homes will thereafter have to pay an annual fee of £150, plus £50 per approved place, over three places [Regulation 5].

Who makes the application?

The application must be made by each person seeking to be registered as:

1.   The person carrying on the business of the care home, and

2.   The manager of the home.

An individual applicant is described as the *responsible person*. In the case of an organisation, s/he is described as the *responsible individual*, and will be a director, manager, secretary or other officer of the organisation running the home.[6] If the owner and the manager are different people, they must *both* be registered, in which case an additional £300 fee will be levied. This will also apply if the manager is the matron, and may well extend to the chief administrator or any other senior person in a position of authority in a larger home. A person who carries on or manages, or wishes to carry on or manage, more than one establishment or agency must make a separate application in respect of each of them.[7]

What must the application contain?

The application must be in writing, on a form approved by the National Care Standards Commission. It must be accompanied by a recent photograph of either the responsible person or the responsible individual.

The application must give detailed information on a number of matters, set out in the regulations, and give any other information that the Commission reasonably requires from the applicant.[8]

The key areas on which information will be sought by the Commission as a requirement of registration are set out in the Registration Regulations (see Appendix One).

There are essentially two categories of information and supporting documents to be provided.

Category one

The first set of information and supporting documents required must be provided by the person who 'carries on the agency', i.e. the owner, or the managing director of the owning company. This person will become the *registered provider*, post registration.[9] The information required is set out in Parts I and II of Schedule 1 of the Registration Regulations, and must be accompanied by the list of documents set out in Schedule 2. Broadly speaking, this information relates to the professional background, employment history, financial experience and probity of the owner, the location and details of the proposed accommodation, the proposed charging scales, the security arrangements, and details about proposed staff, including, where relevant, details of any criminal records (see below).

Category two

The second set of information and supporting documents required must be provided by the person seeking to be the *registered manager* of the care home (who may, of course, be the same person as the registered provider). The information required is set out in Part I of Schedule 3 of the Registration Regulations, and must be accompanied by the list of documents set out in Part II of Schedule 3. This information is all contained in the Appendix to this handbook. Broadly speaking, this information relates to the professional background, relevant qualifications, employment history, health and suitability of the proposed registered manager for the post.

In both categories at least two independent references will be required.

Finally, the application must contain the further information requested in Schedule 4 of the Registration Regulations, stating:

- Details of the accommodation available for residents and persons working in the care home.
- Whether it is proposed to provide nursing care at the care home.
- Whether it is proposed to provide at the care home accommodation, nursing or personal care to children.
- The maximum number of service users for whom the care home is proposed to be used, and the number of such users by reference to their sex, and the categories of old age (if not falling in any other category, with a special category of those also over 65); mental disorder past or present; alcohol or drug dependence past or present; physical disability; children.

What about any criminal records of staff?

Normally criminal convictions that are 'spent' (i.e. a statutory length of time has elapsed since the offence was committed/sentence was completed) should not be referred to in any subsequent transaction.[10] This is based upon the principle contained in the Rehabilitation of Offenders Act 1974, that, subject to certain important exceptions covering very serious offences, every convicted person has a right to rehabilitation. Although this legislation was designed to allow convicted persons to achieve total rehabilitation after a fixed length of time following the end of their sentence, and to be relieved of the need to declare the existence of any minor convictions, there is an important exception as far as employees in care homes are concerned. Any care home employee who may be providing health or social services to a resident is obliged by law to reveal details of any criminal conviction, if asked to do so by, or on behalf of, their employer, as part of the assessment of their suitability for employment in the care home. They cannot use the Rehabilitation of Offenders Act 1974 as a grounds for refusing to reveal convictions that for any other purposes are considered 'spent'.[11]

What happens if changes occur in the care home, after the application has been submitted, whilst awaiting the decision of the National Care Standards Commission on registration?

If any of the following changes occur after the application is made and before the outcome is determined, the applicant has a duty to inform the Commission of the nature and the detail of the changes:[12]

- Change in the name or address of the applicant, or any responsible person.
- If the applicant is a partnership, any change of membership in the partnership.
- (If the applicant is an organisation) any change of director, manager, secretary or other person responsible for the management of the organisation.
- Similar duties to inform will arise if a person is engaged to work at the establishment between application and determination of the outcome.[13]

What happens once the application has been made?

Having received the written application, the Commission will examine the documentation with care and will interview all persons seeking registration, to determine whether the applicant is fit to carry on, or manage, the establishment.[14]

Once they have completed all their enquiries and investigations the Commission will then either register or reject the application. *The burden of proof in establishing that the care home should be registered is with the applicant, not with the registration authority.* Registration may be either unconditional or subject to any such conditions as the registration authority thinks fit.[15] This clearly leaves it open to the Commission to impose a range of specific requirements on a particular home. On granting the application, the Commission will issue a certificate of registration to the applicant. The Commission keeps a register in respect of each care home that they have registered.[16] It seems that some, though not currently all, of the details of each home that are contained in the register will be made available to the public.

CANCELLATION OF REGISTRATION

Can the National Care Standards Commission cancel the registration?

The Commission may at any time cancel[17] the registration of a person in respect of a care home:

(a) on the ground that that person has been convicted of a relevant offence;[18]

(b) on the ground that any other person has been convicted of such an offence in relation to the establishment or agency;

(c) on the ground that the establishment or agency is being, or has at any time been, carried on otherwise than in accordance with the relevant requirements;[19]

(d) on any ground specified by regulations, currently *either* that the registered person has failed to pay at the time prescribed the annual registration fee,[20] *or* that s/he has made a false statement or provided false information in relation to a registration application, *or* that the establishment has ceased to be financially viable, or is likely to cease to be financially viable within the next six months.[21]

The above grounds for cancellation appear to be very comprehensive.

Can the registered person apply for the cancellation of registration?

Registered persons may apply for the cancellation of their registration.[22] They cannot, however, make such an application if the Commission has already given them notice of a proposal to cancel the registration, unless the Commission has subsequently decided not to take this step. Nor may such an application be made if (a) the Commission has given notice to the applicant of their decision to cancel registration; and (b) either the time within which an appeal may be brought has not yet expired, or an appeal has been brought and not yet been determined.[23]

Any application to the Commission for cancellation of registration must be made not less than three months before the proposed effective date, or such shorter period (if any) before that date as may be agreed with the Commission.[24]

What information must the application by a registered provider to cancel their registration contain?

The application to cancel must be accompanied by the following specific information:[25]

(a) The proposed effective date.[26]

(b) A statement as to the arrangements (if any) that have been made by the registered person to ensure that on and after the date of application for cancellation, and the proposed effective date, residents will continue to be provided with similar accommodation (if any) and services, as those provided to them in the care home at the date on which the application for cancellation is made.

(c) The registered person's reasons for making the application for cancellation.

(d) Particulars of any notice of application for cancellation that has been given to any care home residents or their representatives, and to the health authority and the local authority in which the home is situated.

(e) If the registered person has not given notice of their intention to cancel registration to any of the above groups or individuals, a statement explaining whether there were any

> circumstances preventing them from giving, or making it impractical for them to give, such notice of their intention.

If the application is for cancellation less than three months before the proposed effective date, the registered person must also provide a report as to whether the establishment has ceased, or is likely to cease within the following 12 months, to be financially viable.

Is there an urgent procedure for cancellation/amendment of registration?

The Commission may apply to a Justice of the Peace (JP) for an order, either to cancel the registration of a person in respect of a care home; or to vary or remove any condition for the time being in force; or to impose an additional condition.[27] If upon hearing this application it appears to the JP that, unless the order is made, there will be a serious risk to a person's life, health or well-being, s/he may make the order, and the cancellation, variation, removal or imposition shall have effect from the time when the order is made. An application under this procedure may, if the JP thinks fit, be made without notice. As soon as practicable after the making of an application under this provision the Commission must notify the appropriate authorities of the making of the application. Any order made under this provision must be in writing. Where such an order is made, the Commission shall, as soon as practicable after the making of the order, serve on the person registered in respect of the care home a copy of the order and notice of the right of appeal.[28]

VARIATION AND REMOVAL OF CONDITIONS

Applications by registered persons for variation or removal of conditions

The Commission may, at any time after registration, vary or remove any condition for the time being in force in relation to a person's registration, or impose an additional condition.[29]

A person already registered under the Act may apply to the Commission for the variation or removal of any condition, for the time being in force, in relation to the registration.[30]

An application under these provisions must be made in writing on a form approved by the Commission, and must be sent or delivered to the Commission not less than ten weeks before the proposed effective date, or such shorter period (if any) before that date, as may be agreed with the Commission.[31]

The application must be accompanied by the prescribed fee (£550 in the case of an application by a registered provider, £300 if by a registered manager [Regulation 4]) together with information as to the proposed effective date, the registered person's reasons for making the application, and details of changes they propose to make in relation to the establishment as a consequence of the variation or removal of the condition, including details of any proposed structural changes to the premises, and details of any additional staff, facilities or equipment, or management changes.[32]

Rights of appeal are dealt with in Chapter Eight.

INSPECTION

> Inspection should be a well-managed, open process, not a one-off event. It can – and quickly does – become institutionalised in the ways that some (care) homes are institutionalised. If inspection becomes too much of a routine – a chore for both sides to get through as soon as possible – it loses its creative potential for helping (care) homes to bring about change.[33]

The Commission may, at any time, require a person who carries on, or manages, a care home to provide it with any information relating to the care home which it considers it necessary or expedient to have for the purposes of fulfilling its inspection functions.[34] To this end any person authorised by the Commission to act as an inspector may at any time enter and inspect premises which are used, or which it has reasonable cause to believe are being used, as a care home. These inspectors will be trained through a common programme of national competencies, over a period of time, linked to a national award.[35] The inspection frequencies are set out in regulations, and will average two a year.[36] The model comprises a mixture of announced inspections, unannounced inspections and follow-up inspections. The inspectors are trying to achieve a common approach to inspection across all three sectors – public, private and voluntary.

As a rule of thumb, a properly executed announced inspection should take place over about a three-month period, giving the home at least a month's notice of the visit.[37] By its very nature, an unannounced visit will follow a different pattern. An inspector has the powers to do any of the following:[38]

1. Make any examination into the state and management of the premises and treatment of patients or persons accommodated or cared for there, which s/he thinks appropriate.

2. Inspect and take copies of any documents or records (other than medical records) required to be kept in accordance with the

regulations. This includes the power to require the manager or the registered provider to produce any documents or records, wherever kept, for inspection on the premises, and in relation to records which are kept by means of a computer, the power to require the records to be produced in a form in which they are legible and can be taken away.

3. Interview in private the manager or the registered provider, any person employed there, and any patient or person accommodated or cared for there, who consents to be interviewed.

4. If the inspector is either a medical practitioner or a registered nurse, and s/he has reasonable cause to believe that a patient, or a person accommodated or cared for there is not receiving proper care, the inspector may with the consent of that person, examine him/her in private and inspect any medical records relating to his/her treatment in that establishment. These powers may be exercised in relation to a person who is incapable of giving consent, without that person's consent.

5. Any inspector may seize and remove any document or other material or thing found in the course of the inspection, if s/he reasonably believes this may constitute evidence of a failure to comply with any condition or requirement of this part of the Act. The inspector may take any such measurement and photographs, and make any such recordings as s/he considers necessary to exercise his/her powers.[39]

Once the inspector has completed the investigation, s/he must prepare a report on the matters inspected and send a copy of the report to the registered provider, without delay.[40] In addition the Commission must make copies of the inspection report available at its offices, for any person to read at any reasonable time, and must provide a copy of the report, with or without reasonable charge, to any person who requests a copy.[41] The Commission may also take any other steps to publicise a report where it considers such a step to be appropriate.

If any regulations are not complied with on inspection, the Commission should agree actions and a timescale with the provider for compliance to be achieved. This should be reviewed at the end of the period, through a follow up visit. If compliance is not achieved at the end of the period then the Commission will need to prosecute (if a breach of the relevant regulation is an offence) or consider other enforcement action.[42]

Finally, it should be noted that the Commission inspectors will be assisted in their work by lay assessors, which will allow a range of specific and specialised issues to be identified, for example the need to involve relatives and friends fully in the processes of the home. (For further information on the important role of relatives and friends in improving the quality and accountability of the care home, contact the Relatives and Residents Association, 5 Tavistock Place, London WC1H 9SN.)

COURT INTERVENTIONS

A number of specific criminal offences exist in relation to the running of a care home. Note, however, that a criminal conviction under any of the following offences does not automatically disqualify a manager from continuing in his/her position as manager. Also, it should be noted that, in practice, prosecutions in connection with regulatory breaches have been very rare. In the year 1999–2000, only 30 prosecutions were initiated.[43]

1. Failing to register

A person guilty of an offence under this section shall be liable, on summary conviction, either to a fine not exceeding £5000 or (for a repeat offence) to imprisonment for a term not exceeding six months, or to a fine of £5000, or both.[44]

2. Failing to comply with conditions[45]

If a registered provider fails, without reasonable excuse, to comply with any condition for the time being in force in respect of the care home, s/he shall be guilty of an offence and liable on summary conviction to a fine not exceeding £5000.

3. Contravention of regulations[46]

The regulations provide that a contravention of, or failure to comply with specific identified regulations is an offence. A person guilty of such an offence is liable on summary conviction to a fine not exceeding £2500. The regulations covered by these provisions are as follows: Care Homes Regulations 4, 5, 11–26, 37–40.[47] Note that the Commission cannot bring proceedings for contravention of a regulation unless it has first served on the registered person a notice specifying the nature of the alleged breach, what action is needed to remedy it, the time required for compliance (which must not exceed three months); and, unless the period specified in the notice has expired, and the person has contravened or failed to comply with any of the regulations mentioned in the notice.[48]

4. False descriptions of establishments and agencies[49]

A person who, with intent to deceive any person, applies any name to premises in England or Wales, or in any way describes such premises or holds such premises out, so as to indicate, or reasonably be understood to indicate, that the premises constitute a care home, shall be liable on summary conviction to a fine not exceeding £5000 unless registration has been effected under this Part in respect of the premises as a care home.

5. False statements in application[50]

Any person who, in an application for registration, or for the variation of any condition in force in relation to his/her registration, knowingly makes a statement which is false or misleading in a material respect shall be guilty of an offence. A person guilty of an offence under this section shall be liable on summary conviction to a fine not exceeding £2500.

6. Failing to display a certificate of registration[51]

A certificate of registration issued in respect of a care home shall be kept affixed in a conspicuous place in the home. If this requirement is not complied with, the registered provider shall be guilty of an offence and liable on summary conviction to a fine not exceeding £500.

7. Intentional obstruction of inspection[52]

If any person intentionally obstructs the exercise of any inspection power or fails without reasonable excuse to comply with any reasonable request in relation to these powers, s/he will be guilty of an offence and liable on summary conviction to a fine not exceeding £2500.

8. Offences by bodies corporate[53]

Where any offence is committed by a body corporate (which term includes a local authority), if the offence is proved to have been committed with the consent or connivance of, or to be attributable to any neglect on the part of any director, manager, or secretary of the body corporate, or any person who was purporting to act in any such capacity, s/he (as well as the body corporate) shall be guilty of the offence and shall be liable to be proceeded against and punished accordingly. The reference above to a director, manager or secretary of a body corporate includes a reference to any other similar officer of the body; and where the body is a local authority, to any officer or member of the authority.

Proceedings for any of the above offences may be brought by the Commission within a period of six months from the date on which evidence sufficient in the opinion of the prosecutor to warrant the proceedings came to his/her knowledge; but no such proceedings shall be brought more than three years after the commission of the offence.[54]

9. Special powers for court intervention to compel a person to enter or to leave accommodation

There are three separate sets of circumstances, in which action may be taken to compel an older person to enter residential accommodation (which can include a hospital) without his/her consent:

1. Where the person is deemed to be suffering from a 'mental disability or disorder' under the Mental Health Act 1983, and one of the procedures for committing a mentally disabled person to a mental institution is followed.[55]

2. Where a person is considered by a local authority to be in the above category, under the Mental Health Act 1993, but the alternative of guardianship proceedings[56] is chosen, and the local authority as guardian wishes to place the older person in a particular home. This procedure is rarely used, but could become a more attractive option if the current emphasis on 'community care' is strengthened by further allocation of resources. The Court of Appeal has recently extended the use of this approach to uphold the right of a court to intervene to prevent an 'incapable adult' (in this case a 19-year-old woman with an intellectual age of 5–8 years) from returning to her family home, notwithstanding the wish of her mother, and perhaps of herself, that she should do so: (Re F (Adult Patient) (2000)).[57] In this case the court decided that even though the patient did not fall within the definitions of a person who could be taken into guardianship under the Mental Health Act 1983, the necessity to protect her from an undesirable environment[58] gave the court an inherent jurisdiction to intervene and determine where she should live. It was also decided that such

intervention did not conflict with an individual's right to respect for family life, under Article 8 of the European Convention on Human Rights.[59]

3.   Where a person is 'suffering from grave chronic disease, or is aged, infirm or physically incapacitated, and living in unsanitary conditions', and s/he is not receiving proper care and attention, *and* it is in the interests of that person to be detained either for his/her own good, or because s/he is a serious nuisance to other people, there is a (rarely used) procedure for compulsory removal of the person from his/her home to a place of safety, using the magistrates court.[60]

ENDNOTES

1   s.11(1) CSA.

2   s.11(2) CSA.

3   SI No. 3969.

4   SI No. 3980.

5   The government is proposing to phase in full-cost registration fees over a five-year period, subject to a review after about two years. They estimate that the full cost of registration is in reality 200 per cent higher than the current proposed fees, i.e. *c.* £3000. They have said, in this context: 'We expect funding authorities to pay higher commissioning fees for social care as proprietors pass on increases in regulatory fees to the funding authorities. In this way the burden to providers from increases in regulatory fees will be minimised and the sponsorship of social care and independent healthcare will not be adversely affected. Local authorities and health authorities as the major purchasers of care services will absorb the majority of any increased costs as a result of any significant fee increases. It is proposed that they will be compensated for these additional costs.' *National Care Standards Commission (Registration) Regulations 2001 and 2003, Consultation Document: Regulatory Impact Assessment* (DoH, London, 2001, 2003) paras 10.3–10.4.

6   Registration Regulation 2 (1).

7   s.12(4) CSA.

8   s.12(2) CSA and Registration Regulation 3.

9   Registration Regulation 2 (1).

10   Rehabilitation of Offenders Act 1974 s.1.

11   SI 1975 No. 1023, Schedule 1, Part II, amending s.4(2) Rehabilitaion of Offenders Act 1974.

12   Registration Regulation 6.

13   Registration Regulation 7.

14   Registration Regulation 5.

15   s.13(3) CSA.

16   The details of what particulars must appear on a Certificate are contained in Regulation 9 of the Registration Regulations (see Appendix One).

17   Registration Regulation 14.

18   For the purposes of this section the following are relevant offences: (a) an offence under this Part of the Care Standards Act or Regulations made under it; (b) an offence under the Registered Homes Act 1984 or Regulations made under it; (c) an offence under the 1989 Children Act or Regulations made under it.

19   In this section 'relevant requirements' means (a) any requirements or conditions imposed by or under this Part; and (b) the requirements of any other enactment which appear to the National Care Standards Commission to be relevant.

20   s.16(3) CSA.

21   Registration Regulation 14.

22   s.15(1)(b) CSA and Registration Regulation 15.

23   s.15(2) CSA.

24   Registration Regulation 14.

25   Registration Regulation 15 (4).

26   This means the date requested by the registered person as the date on which the cancellation applied for is to take effect: Registration Regulation 15 (1).

27   s.20 CSA.

28   Conferred by s.21 CSA.

29   s.13(5) CSA.

30   s.15 CSA.

31   s.12(2) CSA.

32   Registration Regulation 12 (3).

33   Burton, J. (1998) *Managing Residential Care.* London: Routledge, p.237.

34   s.31 CSA.

35   The training procedures are outlined at Chapters One and Nine. See also Chapter One, Note 32.

36   SI No. 3980, Regulation 6.

37   Burton, J. (1998) *Managing Residential Care.* London: Routledge, p.337.

38   s.31 CSA.

39   s.32 CSA.

40   s.32(5) CSA.

41   s.35(6)(7) CSA.

42   Guidance on the Implementation of Regulations, National Minimum Standard by its NCSL, Jan 2002, DOH.

43   *Frequency of Inspection and Regulatory Fees: a Consultation Paper* (DoH, London, 2001) para. 30.

44   s.11(6) CSA. This heavier penalty will also apply if the person was registered in respect of the establishment or agency at a time before the commission of the offence but the registration was cancelled before the offence was committed.

45   s.24 CSA.

46   s.25 CSA.

47   See Chapter Three.

48   Care Homes Regulation 43.

49   s.26 CSA.

50   s.27 CSA.

51   s.28 CSA.

52   s.31(9) CSA.

53   s.30 CSA.

54   s.29 CSA.

55   See generally Mental Health Act 1983 ss.2,3,4,37,135 and 136, and Jones, R. 2001, *The Mental Health Act Manual* (7th Edition). London: Sweet and Maxwell.

56   Mental Health Act 1983 ss.33–4.

57   (2000) 3 CCLR 210.

58   The family home offered a disturbing picture of chronic neglect, a lack of minimum standards of hygiene and cleanliness, a serious lack of adequate parenting, and worrying exposure to those engaged in sexual exploitation and possible sexual abuse.

59   See Chapter Seven pp.110–13.

60   National Assistance Act 1948, s.47.

CHAPTER THREE

The Care Homes Regulations

This chapter sets out the key regulations that place legal obligations upon care home managers in the day-to-day running of their homes. A failure to comply with any of these regulations will render a care home vulnerable to intervention by the National Care Standards Commission, leading ultimately to closure, unless steps are taken by the home managers to ensure compliance. The Care Home Regulations form the basis of the inspections upon which the registration of a home is based, in tandem with the National Minimum Standards, which are described in Chapter Four. Guidance has stated that 'the Commission will not assess whether Regulations are complied with for currently registered services until the first programmed inspection takes place'.[1]

KEY REGULATIONS

Regulation 4: Statement of purpose

The registered person must compile a *statement of purpose*, which is a written statement of the aims and objectives of the care home, the facilities and services which are to be provided to the residents, and specific details on a number of further issues. For further details on the statement of purpose see Chapter Eight at pp.117–18.

Regulation 5: Service user's guide

The registered person must also produce a written guide to the care home, known as the service user's guide. For further detail on the contents of the guide, see Chapter Eight at pp.117–18. Both the statement of purpose and the guide have to be kept under review, and updated when appropriate.[2]

Regulation 7: Fitness of the registered provider

A person shall not carry on a care home unless they are fit to do so. A person is not fit to carry on a care home unless s/he is *either* an individual (carrying on the care home alone or in partnership[3] with one or more other persons) of integrity and good character and physically and mentally fit to carry on the care home, *or* an organisation that has given notice to the Commission of the name, address and position in the organisation of the responsible individual, who is a director, manager, secretary or other officer of the organisation and is responsible for supervising the management of the care home. Full and satisfactory supporting documentation and information must be provided, as specified in Schedule 2.[4]

A person shall not carry on a care home if s/he has been adjudged bankrupt or sequestration of his/her estate has been awarded and (in either case) s/he has not been discharged and the bankruptcy order has not been annulled or rescinded; or s/he has a composition or arrangement with, or granted a trust deed for, his/her creditors and has not been discharged in respect of it. Note that this last provision seems to contradict the underlying raison d'être of voluntary arrangements of this nature which were specifically designed to keep businesses running with the approval of creditors, rather than go into insolvency.

Regulation 8: Appointment of a manager

The registered provider must appoint an individual to manage the care home where there is no registered manager in respect of the care home, if the registered provider is an organisation or partnership and is not a fit person to manage a care home or is not, or does not intend to be, in full-time day-to-day charge of the care home. Where the registered manager proposes to be, is likely to be, or has been absent from the care home for a continuous period of more than 28 days, the registered provider shall appoint an individual to manage the care home during the registered manager's absence. The individual appointed in the above manner shall not manage the care home unless s/he has been registered under the Care Standards Act as a manager of the care home.[5]

Where the registered provider appoints a person to manage the care home s/he must give notice to the Commission of the name of the person so appointed and the date on which the appointment is to take effect.

Regulation 9: Fitness of the registered manager

A person shall not manage a care home unless s/he is fit to do so. S/he is not fit to manage a care home unless s/he is of integrity and good character, and having regard to the size of the care home, the statement of purpose, and the number and needs of the residents, s/he is physically and mentally fit to manage the care home, and has the qualifications, skills and experience necessary for managing the care home. Full and satisfactory supporting documentation and information must be provided, as specified in Schedule 2.[6]

Regulation 10: The general requirements of the registered person

The registered provider and the registered manager shall, having regard to the size of the care home, the statement of purpose, and the number and needs of the service users, carry on or manage the care home (as the case may be) with sufficient care, competence and skill. If the registered provider is an individual, s/he must undertake, from time to time, such training as is appropriate to ensure that s/he has the experience and skills necessary for carrying on the care home. If the registered provider is an organisation or partnership they must ensure that the responsible individual, or one of the partners, undertakes such training, as described later in Chapter Nine.[7]

Regulation 11: Notification of offences

Where the registered person or the responsible individual is convicted of any criminal offence, whether in England and Wales or elsewhere, s/he must forthwith give notice in writing to the Commission of the date and place of the conviction, details of the conviction and the penalty imposed in respect of the offence.

Regulation 12: General provision and conduct

The registered person must ensure that the care home is conducted so as to promote and make proper provision for the health and welfare of residents and to make proper provision for the care and, where appropriate, treatment, education and supervision of the residents.

Taking account of a resident's wishes

The registered person must, for the purposes of providing care and making proper provision for their health and welfare, so far as it is practicable ascertain and take into account residents' wishes and feelings.

Privacy and dignity

The registered person must make suitable arrangements to ensure that the care home is conducted in a manner which respects the privacy and dignity of residents, and with due regard to the sex, religious persuasion, racial origin, and cultural and linguistic background and any disability of the resident.

Relations between staff and residents

The registered provider and registered manager (if any) must, in relation to the conduct of the care home, maintain good personal and professional relationships with each other, with the residents and with the staff, and must encourage and assist staff to maintain good personal and professional relationships with the residents.

Regulation 13: Arrangements for medical treatment

The registered person must make arrangements for each resident to be registered with a general practitioner of his/her choice and to receive, where necessary, treatment, advice and other services from any health care professional. S/he must also make suitable arrangements for the training of staff in first aid.

Handling of medicines in the care home

The registered person must make arrangements for the recording, handling, safekeeping, safe administration and disposal of medicines received into the care home.

Prevention of infection in the care home

The registered person must make suitable arrangements to prevent infection, toxic conditions and the spread of infection at the care home.

Safety of Premises

The registered person shall ensure that all parts of the home to which residents have access are, so far as reasonably practicable, free from hazards to their safety and that all their activities are free from avoidable risks.[8]

Regulation 16: Facilities and services

General responsibilities

The registered person must provide facilities and services to the resident in accordance with their statement of purpose.[10]

Telecommunication facilities

The registered person must, having regard to the size of the care home and the number and needs of the residents, provide, so far as is necessary for the purpose of managing the care home, appropriate telephone facilities and appropriate facilities for communication by fax transmission.

The registered person must also provide telephone facilities which are suitable for the needs of the residents, and make arrangements to enable residents to use such facilities in private.

Room furniture and furnishings

The registered person must provide in rooms occupied by residents, adequate furniture, bedding and other furnishings, including curtains and floor coverings, and equipment, and screens where necessary. At the same time s/he must permit residents, so far as it is practicable to do so, to bring their own furniture and furnishings into the rooms they occupy.

Laundry facilities

The registered provider must arrange for the regular laundering of linen and clothing, and so far as it is practicable to do so, provide adequate facilities for residents to wash, dry and iron their own clothes if they so wish and, for that purpose, must make arrangements for their clothes to be sorted and kept separately.

The preparation, cooking and storage of food and drink

The registered provider must provide sufficient and suitable kitchen equipment, crockery, cutlery and utensils, and adequate facilities for the preparation and storage of food and drink. S/he must provide adequate facilities for residents to prepare their own food and drink and ensure that such facilities are safe for use by residents. S/he must provide, in adequate quantities, suitable, wholesome and nutritious food and drink that is varied and properly prepared and available at such time as may reasonably be required by residents.

Hygiene in the home

After consultation with the environmental health authority, the registered provider must make suitable arrangements for maintaining satisfactory standards of hygiene in the care home. S/he should keep the care home free from offensive odours and make suitable arrangements for the disposal of general and clinical waste.

Handling of a resident's money

The registered provider must provide a place where the money and valuables of all residents may be deposited for safekeeping, and make arrangements for each resident to acknowledge in writing the return to him/her of any money or valuables, so deposited.

Social and cultural activities

The registered provider must consult residents about their social interests, and make arrangements to enable them to engage in local, social and community activities and to visit, or maintain contact or communicate with, their families and friends. Furthermore, the registered provider must consult residents about the programme of activities arranged by or on behalf of the care home and provide facilities for recreation including, having regard to the needs of residents, activities in relation to recreation, fitness and training.

Religious services

The registered person shall ensure that so far as practicable, residents have the opportunity to attend religious services of their choice.

Regulation 17: Records

The registered person must maintain in respect of each resident a record that includes the following information, documents and other records relating to the resident and ensure that the records are kept securely in the care home:[11]

1. Copy of the Regulation 14 Assessment and the Regulation 15 service user's plan.

2. The resident's name, address, date of birth, marital status, his/her photograph, date on which s/he entered [or left] the care home, and whether or not s/he is the subject of any court order.

3.   The name, address and telephone number of the resident's next of kin, and of any person authorised to act on his/her behalf.

4.   The name, address and telephone number of the resident's GP and of any officer of a local social services authority whose duty it is to supervise his/her welfare.

5.   If the resident has been transferred to another care home or to a hospital, the name of the care home or hospital and the date of the transfer.

6.   If the resident died at the care home, the date, time and cause of death.

7.   The name and address of any authority, organisation or other body that arranged the resident's admission to the care home.

8.   A record of all medicines kept in the care home for the resident and the date on which they are administered to the resident.

9.   A record of any accident affecting the resident in the care home and of any other incident in the care home that was detrimental to the health or welfare of the resident. This record must include the nature, date and time of the accident or incident, whether medical treatment was required and the name of the persons who were respectively in charge of the care home and supervising the resident.

10. A record of any nursing provided to the resident, including a record of his/her condition and any treatment or surgical intervention.

11. Details of any specialist communication needs of the resident and methods of communication that may be appropriate for him/her.

12. Details of any plan relating to the resident in respect of medication, nursing, specialist health care or nutrition.

13. A record of incidence of pressure sores and of treatment provided.

14. A record of falls and of treatment provided.

15. A record of any physical restraint used on the resident.

16. A record of any limitations agreed with the resident as to their freedom of choice, liberty of movement and power to make decisions.

17. A copy of all correspondence relating to each resident.

The registered person must also retain in the home the following further records:[12]

General

1. A copy of the statement of purpose, the service user's guide, all inspection reports, and any Regulation 26 report.[13]

2. A record of all accounts kept in the care home.

Individual employees

1. A record of all persons employed at the care home, including their full names, addresses, dates of birth, qualifications and experience.

2. A copy of their birth certificates and passports, of each of their references, the dates on which they commenced or ceased to be employed, the position they hold, the work that they perform, and the number of hours for which they are employed each week.

3. All correspondence, reports, records of any disciplinary action and any other records in relation to their employment.

Duty roster

A copy of the duty roster of persons working at the care home and a record of whether the roster was actually worked.

Money and charging records

A record of the care home's charges to residents, including any extra amounts payable for additional services not covered by those charges, and the amounts paid by or in respect of each resident.

A record of all money or other valuables deposited by a resident for safe-keeping or received on each resident's behalf, stating the date on which the money or valuables were deposited or received, the date on which any money or valuables were returned to a resident, at his/her request or on his/her behalf and, where applicable, the purpose for which the money or valuables were used.

Records shall also include a written acknowledgement of the return of the money or valuables.

Furniture

A record of furniture brought by a resident into the room s/he occupies.

Complaints

A record of all complaints made by residents or their representatives or relatives, or by persons working at the care home about the operation of the care home and the action taken by the registered person in respect of any such complaint.

Visitors

A record of the names of all the visitors to the care home.

Incidents

A record of any of the following events that occur in the care home: any accident; any incident that is detrimental to the health or welfare of a resident, including the outbreak of infectious disease in the care home; any injury or illness; any fire or use of the fire alarm equipment; any theft or burglary. A statement of the procedure to be followed in the event of accidents, or in the event of a resident becoming missing.

Food

Records of the food provided for residents in sufficient detail to enable any person inspecting the record to determine whether the diet is satisfactory, in relation to nutrition and otherwise, and of any special diets prepared for individual residents.

Fire

A record of every fire practice, drill or test of fire equipment (including fire alarms) conducted in the care home and of any action taken to remedy defects in the fire equipment. A statement of the procedure to be followed in the event of a fire, or when a fire alarm is given.

Finally note that the registered person must ensure that all the records referred to above are kept up to date, and are at all times available for inspection in the care home, by any person authorised by the Commission to enter and inspect the care home.

All the records referred to above shall be retained for not less than three years from the date of the last entry.

(For regulations 18 [Staffing] and 19 [Fitness of workers] see Chapter Nine at pp.131–2.)

Regulation 20: Restrictions on acting for a resident

Subject to the next paragraph, the registered person shall not pay money belonging to any resident into a bank account unless the account is in the name of the resident, or any of the residents, to which the money belongs, and the account is not used by the registered person in connection with the carrying on or management of the care home.

The above paragraph does *not* apply to money that is paid to the registered person in respect of charges payable by a resident for accommodation or other services provided by the registered person at the care home.

The registered person must ensure, so far as practicable, that any person working at the care home does not act as the agent of a resident.

Regulation 21: Staff views as to conduct of the care home

This regulation applies to any matter relating to the conduct of the care home so far as it may affect the health or welfare of residents.

The registered person must make arrangements to enable staff to inform the registered person and the Commission of their views about any matter to which this regulation applies.

(For Regulation 22 [Complaints] see Chapter Eight.)

Regulation 23: Fitness of premises for residents and staff

The registered person shall not use premises for the purposes of a care home unless they are fit to be so used. For the purposes of these regulations, premises are not fit to be used as a care home unless they are suitable for the purpose of achieving the aims and objectives set out in the statement of purpose and the location of the premises is appropriate to the needs of residents.

The registered person must, having regard to the number and needs of the service users, ensure that:

1.   the physical design and layout of the premises to be used as the care home meet the needs of the residents;

2.   the premises to be used as the care home are of sound construction and kept in a good state of repair externally and internally;

3.   all parts of the care home are kept clean and reasonably decorated;

4.   equipment provided at the care home for use by residents or staff is maintained in good working order.

5.   adequate private and communal accommodation is provided for residents;

6.   both the size and the layout of rooms occupied or used by residents are suitable for their needs;

7.   there is adequate sitting, recreational and dining space provided separately from the resident's private accommodation;

8.   the communal space provided for residents is suitable for the provision of social, cultural and religious activities appropriate to the circumstances of the residents;

9.   suitable facilities are provided for residents to meet visitors in communal accommodation, and in private accommodation that is separate from the residents' own private rooms;

10.   there are provided at appropriate places in the premises sufficient numbers of lavatories and of wash-basins, baths and showers fitted with a hot- and cold-water supply;

11.   any necessary sluicing facilities are provided;

12.   suitable provision is made for storage for the purposes of the care home;

13.   suitable storage facilities are provided for the use of residents;

14.   suitable adaptations are made, and such support, equipment and facilities, including passenger lifts, as may be required are provided, for residents who are old, infirm or physically disabled;

15.   external grounds that are suitable for, and safe for use by, residents are provided and appropriately maintained;

16.   ventilation, heating and lighting suitable for residents is provided in all parts of the care home which are used by residents;

17.   staff are provided with suitable facilities and accommodation, other than sleeping accommodation, including facilities for the purpose of changing; storage facilities and sleeping accommodation where the provision of such accommodation is needed by staff in connection with their work at the care home.

Fire protection

The registered person shall, after consultation with the fire authority:

1.   take adequate precautions against the risk of fire, including the provision of fire prevention equipment;

2.   provide adequate means of escape;

3.   make adequate arrangements for detecting, containing and extinguishing fires; for giving warnings of fires; for the evacuation, in the event of fire, of all persons in the care home and safe placement of residents; for the maintenance of all fire equipment, and for reviewing fire precautions, and testing fire equipment, at suitable intervals;

4.   make arrangements for persons working at the care home to receive suitable training in fire prevention and ensure, by means of fire drills and practices at suitable intervals, that the persons working at the care home and so far as practicable, the residents themselves, are aware of the procedure to be followed in case of fire, including the procedure for saving life;

5.   undertake appropriate consultation with the authority responsible for environmental health for the area in which the care home is situated.

In addition to all the above requirements, service providers must also ensure that the care home complies with the National Minimum Standards.[14]

Regulation 24: Review of the quality of care

The registered person shall establish and maintain a system for reviewing at appropriate intervals, and improving, the quality of care (including where appropriate of nursing care) at the care home. This system must provide for consultation with residents and their representatives.

The registered person must supply to the Commission a report in respect of any review s/he has conducted under the above paragraph, and make a copy of the report available to residents.

Regulation 25: Financial position of care home

The registered provider shall carry on the care home in such manner as is likely to ensure that the care home will be financially viable for the purpose of achieving the aims and objectives set out in the statement of purpose.

The registered person shall, if the Commission so requests, provide it with such information and documents as it may require in order to consider the financial viability of the care home, including:

(a) the annual accounts of the care home certified by an accountant;

(b) a reference from a bank expressing an opinion as to the registered provider's financial standing;

(c) information as to the financing and financial resources of the care home;

(d) where the registered provider is a company, information as to any of its associated companies;

(e) a certificate of insurance for the registered provider in respect of liability which may be incurred by him/her in relation to the care home in respect of death, injury, public liability, damage or other loss.

The registered person must:

(a) ensure that adequate accounts are maintained in respect of the care home and kept up to date;

(b) ensure that the accounts give details of the running costs of the care home, including rent, payments under a mortgage and expenditure on food, heating and salaries and wages of staff;

(c) supply a copy of the accounts to the Commission at its request.

In this regulation a company is an associated company of another if one of them has control of the other, or both are under the control of the same person.

Regulation 26: Visits by registered provider

Where the registered provider is an individual, but not in day-to-day charge of the care home, s/he must visit the care home in accordance with this regulation. Where the registered provider is an organisation or partnership, the care home shall be visited in accordance with this regulation by the responsible individual, or one of the partners, as the case may be, or *either* another of the directors or other persons responsible for the management of the organisation, *or* an employee of the organisation who is not directly concerned with the conduct of the care home.

The above visits must take place at least once a month and must be unannounced. The person carrying out the visit must interview, with their consent and in private, such of the residents and their representatives and persons working at the care home as appears necessary in order to form an opinion of the standard of care provided in the care home. S/he must also inspect the premises of the care home, its record of events and records of any complaints and prepare a written report on the conduct of the care home.

The registered provider must supply a copy of the above report to the Commission, the registered manager and, where the care home is an organisation (see above), to each of the directors or other persons responsible for the management of the home, or when it is a partnership, to each of the partners.

Regulation 37: Notification of death, illness and other events

The registered person must give notice to the Commission, without delay, of the occurrence of any of the following incidents:

1. The death of any resident and the circumstances of the death.

2. The outbreak in the care home of any infectious disease which in the opinion of any registered medical practitioner attending persons in the care home is sufficiently serious to be so notified.

3. Any serious injury to a resident.

4. Serious illness of a resident at a care home at which nursing is not provided.

5. Any event in the care home that adversely affects the well-being or safety of any resident.

6. Any theft, burglary or accident in the care home.

7. Any allegation of misconduct by the registered person or any person who works at the care home.

Any notification made in accordance with this regulation which is given orally must be subsequently confirmed in writing.

Regulation 38: Notice of absence

Where the registered provider, if an individual, or the registered manager proposes to be absent from the care home for a continuous period of 28 days or more, s/he shall give notice in writing to the Commission of the proposed absence. Except in the case of an emergency, this notice must be given no later than one month before the proposed absence or within such shorter period as may be agreed with the Commission. The notice shall specify the length or expected length of the proposed absence, the reason for that absence, the arrangements that have been made for the running of the care home during that absence, the name, address and qualifications of the person who will be responsible for the care home during that absence and the name, address and qualifications of the person appointed in accordance with Regulation 8, or the arrangements to be made for appointing such a person, if it is the manager who will be absent.

Where the absence arises as a result of an emergency, the registered provider shall give notice of the absence within one week of its occurrence specifying the matters set out above.

Regulation 39: Notice of changes

The registered person must give notice in writing to the Commission as soon as it is practicable to do so if any of the following events takes place or is proposed to take place:

(a) A person other than the registered person is to carry on or manage the care home.

(b) A person ceases to carry on or manage the care home.

(c) Where the registered person is an individual, s/he changes his/her name.

(d) Where the registered provider is a partnership, there is any change in the membership of the partnership.

(e) Where the registered provider is an organisation (i) the name or address of the organisation is changed or (ii) there is any change of director, manager, secretary or other similar officer of the organisation or (iii) there is to be any change of the responsible individual.

(f)   Where the registered provider is an individual, a trustee in bankruptcy is appointed.

(g)   Where the registered provider is a company, or partnership, a receiver, manager, liquidator or provisional liquidaror is appointed.

(h)   The premises of the care home are significantly altered or extended, or additional premises are acquired.

Regulation 40: Notice of termination of accommodation

The registered person must not terminate the arrangements for the accommodation of a resident unless s/he has given *reasonable notice* of his/her intention to that resident, and to the person who appears to be their next of kin and, where a local authority has made arrangements for the provision of accommodation, nursing or personal care to the resident at the care home, to that authority. If it is impracticable for the registered person to comply with the above requirement they must nevertheless do so as soon as it is practicable to do so, and shall provide to the Commission a statement as to the circumstances which made it impracticable for them to comply with the requirement.

Regulation 41: Appointment of liquidators etc.

Any person listed below must immediately notify the Commission of his/her appointment, indicating the reasons for it. S/he must appoint a manager to take full-time day-to-day charge of the care home in any case where there is no registered manager and within 28 days of his/her appointment notify the Commission of his/her intentions regarding the future operation of the care home.

(a)   The receiver or manager of the property of a company or partnership which is a registered provider in respect of a care home.

(b)   A liquidator or provisional liquidator of a company which is a registered provider of a care home

(c)   The trustee in bankruptcy of a registered provider of a care home.

Regulation 42: Death of registered person

If more than one person is registered in respect of a care home and a registered person dies, the surviving registered person shall without delay notify the Commission of the death in writing. If only one person is registered in respect of a care home and that person dies, his/her personal representatives shall, without delay, notify the Commission of the death in writing and within 28 days of their intentions regarding the future running of the home.

(For Regulation 43 [Offences] see Chapter Two at pp.30–33.)

Regulation 44: Compliance with regulations

Where there is more than one registered person in respect of a care home, anything which is required under these regulations to be done by the registered person shall, if done by one of the registered persons, not be required to be done by any of the other registered persons.

Regulation 45: Adult placements

A *registered provider* is an 'adult placement carer' in respect of a care home if:

(a) s/he is the registered provider in respect of, and s/he manages, the care home; *and*

(b) no person other than the registered provider manages the care home; *and*

(c) the care home is, or forms part of their home, or the home where they ordinarily reside; *and*

(d) no more than three residents are accommodated in the 'care home'; *and*

(e) a placement agreement[15] has been made in respect of each of the residents; *and*

(f) each service user is over the age of 18.

Many of the regulations do not apply, or apply less stringently, to registered providers. The detail of these modifications is set out in Regulation 46.

ENDNOTES

1   *Guidance on the Implementation of Regulations and National Minimum Standards by the NCSC,* Jan 2002, DoH.

2   Care Homes Regulations 2001, Regulation 6.

3   If a partnership: *each* of the partners must satisfy these requirements. Regulation 7(2)(a)(ii).

4   This includes proof of identity, photograph, birth certificate, current passport (if any), documentary evidence of relevant qualifications, two written references, and evidence that they are physically and mentally fit to do the job.

5   See Chapter Two at pp.21–22.

6   See Note 4.

7   See Chapter Nine at pp.132–5.

8   Detailed guidance in this respect can be found in the Health and Safety Publication 'Health and Safety in Care Homes,' 2001 (ref HSG 220).

9   For more of the Assessment Process for Admission to Care Homes, see Chapter Five.

10 See Chapter Eight at p.117–8.

11 Schedule 2 to the Care Homes Regulations 2001.

12 Schedule 3 to the Care Homes Regulations 2001.

13 See below at p.51.

14 See Chapter Four.

15 A 'placement agreement' is an agreement between a registered provider, a resident and a local authority or other body managing an adult placement scheme. The agreement will contain details of the room(s) to be occupied by and services provided to the proposed user, the fees to be charged, and details of the qualifications and experience of the registered provider, plus any other proposed terms and conditions.

CHAPTER FOUR

The National Minimum Standards

PURPOSE OF THE STANDARDS

The National Minimum Standards[1] apply to 'all care homes providing accommodation and nursing or personal care for older people'. They do not however apply to independent hospitals, hospices, clinics or establishments registered to take patients detained under the Mental Health Act 1983. National Minimum Standards for these services are being separately developed.[2] The Minister must keep the Standards under review. Before issuing an amending statement which in his or her opinion effects a substantial change in the Standards, the Minister must consult any 'appropriate persons'.

The Standards are intended to form the central framework of the new regulatory framework.[3] They must however be read in conjunction with the Regulations described in Chapters Two and Three, as in a number of cases the Standards do little more than reiterate the legal duties already imposed upon care home managers and providers by virtue of the Regulations. And, unlike directions or regulations, standards are not legally binding,[4] although they must be 'taken into account',[5] and a breach of any standard may be a reason to refuse, qualify, or withdraw registration.

In the Introduction to the Standards framework document itself, the proposed function of the Standards is explained in the following terms:

1. The Act gives powers to the Secretary of State to publish statements of National Minimum Standards that the National Care Standards Commission must take into account when making its decisions.

2. These Standards will form the basis for judgements made by the Commission regarding registration and the imposition of conditions for registration, variation of any conditions and enforcement of compliance with the Care Standards Act and

associated regulations, including proceedings for cancellation of registration or prosecution.

3.   The Commission will therefore consider the degree to which a regulated service complies with the Standards when determining whether or not a service should be registered or have its registration cancelled, or whether to take any action for breach of regulations.

According to the Preamble to the Standards,[6] they focus on:

Achievable outcomes for service users, i.e. the impact on the individual of the facilities and services of the home. Regulators will look for evidence that the facilities, resources, policies, activities and services of the home lead to positive outcomes for, and the active participation of, service users.

In addition they are designed to ensure that:

1.   care home managers, staff and premises are 'fit for their purpose';

2.   The home comprehensively meets the assessed needs of each individual living there, and that changing needs continue to be comprehensively met;

3.   The home demonstrates a commitment to continuous improvements, thereby assuring a good quality of life and health for service users;

4.   The home staff are all adequately trained according to the requirements of the National Training Organisation for the Personal Social Services (TOPSS), and the Code of Practice published by the General Social Care Council.

The Standards are grouped under seven heads, known as the 'key topics' as follows:

1.   Choice of Home: Standards 1–6

2.   Health and Personal Care: Standards 7–11

      (These are dealt with in Chapter Six)

3.   Daily Life and Social Activities: Standards 12–15

4.   Complaints and Protection: Standards 16–18

      (These are dealt with in Chapter Eight)

5.   Environment: Standards 19–26

6.   Staffing: Standards 27–30

7.   Management and Administration: Standards 31–38

Each 'key topic' is prefaced by a statement of good practice, which sets out the rationale for the standard in question, and a statement of the intended *outcome* for residents to be achieved by the care home. The standards are intended to be measurable.

In its inspections, the National Care Standards Commission will look for evidence that the requirements are being met and that a good quality of life is being enjoyed by the residents. To find this evidence it will use the following methods: discussions with residents, their families and friends, staff managers and others; observation of daily life in the home; scrutiny of written policies, procedures and records.

NOTE ON TERMINOLOGY AND TIMING

Terminology. In law, 'service user' means 'any person who is to be provided with accommodation or services in an establishment or by an agency'.[7] The term 'service user' is used throughout the Standards, as it is in the Care Standards Act and the Regulations. But as care home staff will normally see this term as synonymous with the word 'resident', I have adopted the term 'resident' throughout this chapter, in preference to 'service user'.

Timing. The great majority of these standards are effective from April 2002. Where in a few limited cases their introduction has been delayed to a later date this is indicated with italics. This will include circumstances where the standard will only be applied to new-build homes, and to first-time registrations.

CHOICE OF HOME: 1–6

Standard 1

Outcome. Prospective residents will have the information they need to make an informed choice about where they live.

Process. Provide a user guide written in plain English (and other appropriate formats) which will include details about the qualifications and experience of the manager and staff, of the accommodation and services provided, including meeting special needs and interests, a copy of the most recent inspection report, a sample of residents' views about the home, and a copy of the complaints procedure. For more information on the user's guide see Chapter 8 at pp.117–8.

Standard 2

Outcome: Each resident will have a written contract/statement of terms and conditions with the home.

Process: Prepare in advance a document to include details of rooms to be occupied, the rights and obligations of both user and provider, the terms and conditions of the occupancy, who is to pay the fee, what is covered by the fee, what happens in the case of a breach of the contract, and what additional services are available at extra cost.

Standard 3

Outcome: No resident will move into the home without having had his/her needs assessed and having been assured that these needs will be met.

Process: Ensure that a full care assessment has been carried out on individuals by a registered professional person, before they are admitted to the care home, and the care home is satisfied that it will be able to meet these assessed needs in full. Attached to each care assessment there must be a care plan, including where necessary a plan for nursing care (see Standard 7).

Standard 4

Outcome: Residents and their representatives must know that the home they enter will meet their needs.

Process: Demonstrate that any care services that the care home provides to meet assessed need are based upon current good practice, and that the staff collectively have the skills and experience to deliver the services. In addition they must be able to demonstrate that any specific needs and preferences will be met (for example, special religious or culturally based requirements).

Standard 5

Outcome: Prospective residents and their relatives and friends will have an opportunity to visit and to assess the quality, facilities and suitability of the home.

Process: The care home must give prospective residents the opportunity to visit the home, and if appropriate, to move into the home on a trial basis. In the case of emergency admissions, the home must inform the resident within 48 hours about key aspects, rules and routines of the service, and meet all other admission criteria set out in Standards 2–4 within 5 working days.

Standard 6

Outcome: Service users who have been assessed and referred solely for intermediate care[8] will be helped to maximise their independence and return home.

Process: Dedicated accommodation, together with specialised facilities, equipment and staff must be provided that will deliver short-term intensive rehabilitation, enabling the service user to return home.

(For information on Health and Personal Care: 7–11, see Chapter Five.)

DAILY LIFE AND SOCIAL ACTIVITIES: 12–15

Standard 12

Outcome: Residents find that the lifestyle and activities made available are flexible and varied to suit their expectations, preferences and capacities.

Process: The care home must ensure that residents are offered variety, and are able to exercise choice, in relation to their leisure and social activities, their cultural interests, their food, meals and mealtimes, the routines of their daily living, in their personal and social relationships, and in their religious observances. There must be evidence that residents' interests are recorded, and information about available activities is made widely available to residents, in accessible formats.

Standard 13

Outcome: Residents maintain contact with family, friends, representatives and the local community as they wish.

Process: Residents should be able to receive visitors in private and to choose whom they do and do not see. Involvement in the home by local community groups and/or volunteers should accord with residents' preferences.

Standard 14

Outcome: Residents are helped to exercise choice and control over their lives.

Process: This standard can be demonstrated by a range of processes (e.g. autonomy to handle own financial affairs, right to bring personal possessions into the home when joining) that collectively provide evidence that the home is committed to maximising each resident's capacity to exercise personal autonomy and choice.

Standard 15

Outcome: Residents receive a wholesome, appealing and balanced diet in pleasing surroundings at times convenient to them.

Process: A number of fairly prescriptive measures are set out in the document as providing the means of achieving this particular standard. For example, each resident should be offered three full meals a day, that are attractive and appealingly presented, at least one of which should be cooked, at intervals of not more than five hours. Hot and cold drinks should be available at all times and offered regularly. Religious, cultural or therapeutic dietary requirements should be observed. Menus should be varied and changed regularly. Mealtimes should be unhurried. Discreet assistance should be available in assisting eating, if required.

(For information on Complaints and Protection: 16–18, see Chapter Eight.)

ENVIRONMENT: 19–26 (to be relaxed from 1/3/03, see www.carestandards.org.uk)

Standard 19

Outcome: Residents live in a safe, well-maintained environment.

Process: There must be in place a programme of routine maintenance, including renewal of the fabric and decoration of the premises, and tidying and maintenance of the grounds, to ensure that the residents live in such an environment. The building must comply with all relevant fire and environmental health requirements. CCTV must be limited to entrance areas for security purposes.

Standard 20

Outcome: Residents have access to safe and comfortable indoor and outdoor communal facilities.

Process: The home must provide sitting, recreational and dining space amounting to at least 4.1 sq m for each service user. This must include a smoke-free sitting room, a dining room to cater for all service users, and other rooms in which a variety of social, cultural and religious activities can take place, and in which residents can meet visitors in private. Lighting must be bright, and furnishing 'domestic in character' and of good quality. In addition, there must be outdoor space, accessible to wheelchair users and those with other mobility problems, and designed to meet the needs of those with physical, sensory and cognitive impairment. *This standard will not be applied to homes existing prior to 1.4.02, until 1.4.07.* 'Existing homes' includes local authority homes in existence prior to April 2002.

Standard 21

Outcome: Residents have sufficient and suitable lavatories and washing facilities.

Process: There must be clearly marked, accessible toilets for residents, close to the lounge and dining areas, and each resident must have a toilet within close proximity to his/her private accommodation. There should be a ratio of one assisted bath to eight service users. This ratio should be interpreted flexibly with disabled showers being considered as an assisted bath. The overall quality of care, and architectural constraints, can be taken into account. Guidance urges the Commission to consult an occupational therapist in difficult cases. Where suitably adapted ensuite/bathing/shower facilities are provided in a resident's rooms, these rooms will be excluded from the calculation. *Ensuite facilities (a minimum of a toilet and a handbasin) must be provided to all residents in all new-build, extensions and all first-time registrations from 1.4.02.*

Standard 22

Outcome: Residents have the specialist equipment they require to maximise their independence.

Process: The home must be able to demonstrate that an assessment of the premises and facilities has been made by suitably qualified persons, including a qualified occupational therapist, with specialist knowledge of the client groups catered for, and provides evidence that the recommended disability equipment has been secured or provided and environmental adaptations made to meet the needs of service users.

Service users must have access to all their communal and private space, through the provision of ramps and passenger lifts,[9] if they are required to achieve such access. The home should provide grab rails and other aids in corridors, bathrooms, toilets, communal rooms and where necessary in the residents' own accommodation. In addition aids, hoists and assisted toilets and baths must be installed if necessary to meet the assessed needs of a resident. Doorways into communal areas, residents' rooms, bathing and toilet facilities and other spaces to which wheelchair users have access, must all have a clear opening width of 800mm.[10] Facilities, including communication aids such as a loop system, and signs should be provided to assist the needs of residents, taking account of the needs, for example, of those with hearing impairment, visual impairment, dual sensory impairments, learning disabilities or dementia or other cognitive impairment, where necessary.

Storage areas should be provided for aids and equipment, including wheelchairs. A call system with an accessible alarm facility should be provided in every room.

Standard 23

Outcome: Residents' own rooms suit their needs.

Process: The home must provide accommodation for each resident which meets minimum space requirements as follows:

1. *In all new-build, extensions and first-time registrations, all places provided in single rooms must offer a minimum of 12 sq m usable floorspace (excluding ensuite[11] facilities).*

2. *Single rooms in current use must have at least 10 sq m usable floor space (excluding ensuite facilities) from 1 April 2007. From 1 April 2007, existing single rooms which fall below the 10 sq m standard, but are no lower than 9.3 sq m, will only be permitted if other compensatory quality standards are present as follows: additional communal space made available for private use, or ensuite facilities in the single rooms in question.*

3. Single rooms accommodating wheelchair users must have at least 12 sq m usable floorspace (excluding ensuite facilities).

4. Room dimensions and layout options must ensure that there is room on either side of the bed, to enable access for carers and any equipment needed.[12]

5. Where rooms are shared, they must be occupied by no more than two service users who have made a positive choice to share with each other. When a shared place becomes vacant, the remaining service user should be given the opportunity to choose not to share, by moving into a different room if necessary.

6. Rooms that are currently shared must have at least 16 sq m of usable floor space (excluding ensuite facilities).

7. *In new-build, extensions and all first-time registrations, residents wishing to share accommodation must be offered two single rooms for use, for example, as bedroom and sitting room.*

8. *From 1 April 2007, existing homes that do not already provide 80 per cent of places in single rooms must do so. 'Existing homes' includes local authority homes.*

Standard 24

Outcome: Residents live in safe, comfortable bedrooms with their own possessions around them.

Process: The home should provide private accommodation for each service user that is furnished and equipped to assure comfort and privacy, and meets the assessed needs of the service user. In the absence of a resident's own provision, furnishings for individual rooms must be provided to the minimum as follows:

- a clean comfortable bed, minimum 900mm wide, at a suitable, safe height for the resident, plus bed-linen;
- curtains or blinds;
- a mirror;
- overhead and bedside lighting;
- comfortable seating for two people;
- drawers and enclosed space for hanging clothes;
- at least two accessible double electric sockets;
- a table to sit at and a bedside table;
- a wash hand basin (unless ensuite WC and basin provided).

In addition, each room should be carpeted, or equivalent. Doors to residents' private accommodation should be fitted with locks suited to their capabilities and accessible to staff in emergencies. Residents should be provided with their own keys unless their risk assessment suggests otherwise. They should also have lockable storage space for medication, money and valuables and be provided with a key they can retain (unless the reason for not doing so is explained in the care plan). Adjustable beds must be provided for residents receiving nursing care. In double rooms screening should be provided to ensure privacy for personal care.

Standard 25

Outcome: Residents live in safe, comfortable surroundings.

Process: The heating, lighting, water supply and ventilation of the accommodation should meet the relevant environmental health and safety requirements, and the needs of individual service users. Rooms should be individually and naturally ventilated with windows conforming to recognised standards. *In new-build, extensions and all first-time registrations the height of the window should enable a resident to see out of it when seated or in bed.* Rooms should be centrally heated and heating controllable in the resident's own room. Any pipework and radiators should be guarded or have guaranteed low temperature surfaces. Lighting in a resident's accommodation should meet recognised standards (lux 150), be domestic in character, and include table-level lamp lighting. Emergency lighting should be provided throughout the home. Water should be stored at a temperature of at least 60 °C and distributed at 50 °C minimum, to prevent risks from Legionella. To prevent risks from scalding, pro-set valves of a type unaffected by changes in water pressure and with fail-safe devices should be fitted locally to provide water close to 43 °C.

Standard 26

Outcome: The home is clean, pleasant and hygienic.

Process: The premises should be kept clean, hygienic and free from offensive odours throughout and systems put in place to control the spread of infection, in accordance with relevant legislation and published professional guidance. All laundry facilities should be sited so that soiled articles, clothing and infected linen are not carried through areas where food is stored, prepared, cooked or eaten and do not intrude on the residents. Hand-washing facilities should be prominently sited in areas where infected material and/or clinical waste are being handled. The laundry floor finishes should be impermeable and, together with wall finishes, readily cleanable. Policies and procedures for control of infection should include the safe handling and disposal of clinical waste, dealing with spillages, provision of protective clothing and hand-washing.

The home should have a sluicing facility and, in care homes providing nursing, a sluicing disinfector. All foul laundry should be washed at appropriate temperatures (minimum 65°C for not less than 10 minutes) to thoroughly clean linen and control risk of infection. Washing machines should have the specified programming ability to meet disinfection standards. Services and facilities must all comply with the Water Supply (Water Fittings) Regulations 1999.

STAFFING: 27–30

Standard 27

Outcome: Residents' needs are met by the number and skill mix of staff.

Process: The care home must maintain a recorded staff rota showing which staff are on duty at any time, day and night, and in what capacity. The staff/resident ratio must be in accordance with DoH guidance. Additional staff must be on duty at peak times of the day. Staff providing personal care must be at least 18,[13] and those left in charge of the home at least 21. Domestic staff must be employed in sufficient numbers to ensure that standards relating to meals, food, nutrition, hygiene and cleanliness are met.

Standard 28

Outcome: Residents are in safe hands at all times.[14]

Process: By 2005, a minimum ratio of 50% trained members of care staff (NVQ level 2 or equivalent) must be achieved, excluding the registered manager and/or care manager, and in care homes providing nursing, excluding those members of the care staff who are registered nurses.[15] Trainees, including all staff under 18, must be registered on a TOPSS-certified training programme.

Standard 29

Outcome: Residents are supported and protected by the home's recruitment policy and practices.

Process: The care home must operate a recruitment procedure based upon equal opportunities, and ensuring the protection of residents, in accordance with the General Social Care Council (GSCC) code of conduct and practice.[16] Two written references must be obtained before appointing a member of staff, and any gaps in employment records must be explored. The recruitment and selection process for volunteers must be thorough and include police checks. All staff should be given a statement of the terms and conditions of their employment, and of the GSCC code of conduct and practice.

Standard 30

Outcome: Staff are trained and competent to do their jobs.

See Chapter Eight.[17]

MANAGEMENT AND ADMINISTRATION: 31–38

Standard 31

Outcome: Residents live in a home which is run and managed by a person who is fit to be in charge, of good character and able to discharge his/her responsibilities fully.

Process: The registered manager must have at least two years' experience in a senior management capacity in the managing of a relevant care setting within the past five years, and *(by 2005) either a qualification at level 4 NVQ in management and care or equivalent, or where nursing care is provided by the home be a first-level registered nurse, and have a relevant management qualification.* The registered manager must be responsible for no more than one registered establishment, and able to demonstrate that s/he has undertaken periodic training to update his/her knowledge, skills and competence, whilst managing the home.

Standard 32

Outcome: Residents benefit from the ethos, leadership and management approach of the home.

Process: The registered manager must ensure that the management approach of the home creates an open, positive, transparent and inclusive atmosphere, and that there are in place strategies for enabling staff, residents and 'other stakeholders' to affect the way in which the service is delivered, and encouraging innovation, creativity and development.

Standard 33

Outcome: The home is run in the best interests of the residents.

Process: The home must have an annual development plan, based upon a systematic cycle of planning, action, review, reflecting aims and outcomes for service users, with continuous self-monitoring. Policies, procedures and practices must be regularly reviewed in the light of new legislation and practice guidance and advice. Residents and their families and friends must be involved as stakeholders, and included in activities in the review and inspection process.

Standard 34

Outcome: Residents are safeguarded by the accounting and financial procedures of the home.

Process: Safeguarding should include insurance against loss or damage to the assets of the building, for business interruption costs, as well as costs to the operator of meeting contract liabilities. There must be in place a business and financial plan for the establishment that is open to inspection and reviewed annually.

Standard 35

Outcome: Residents' financial interests are safeguarded.

Process: Written records of all transactions must be maintained. Personal allowances of residents must not be pooled. Secure facilities must be provided for safekeeping of money and valuables belonging to residents. The registered manager can be appointed as agent for a resident only where no other individual is available, subject to clear written procedures and safeguards.

In addition to the above procedures, it should also be noted that a number of further procedures are available to assist in the management of the finances of a resident who can no longer manage his or her own finances, as follows:

Appointees

If a resident is entitled to benefits, and cannot act for him/herself, s/he can appoint someone aged 18 or over to act on his/her behalf. An appointee is usually a friend or relative, but can be anybody, including for example a bank manager, a solicitor, or (in theory) a care home manager. This Standard is however concerned that care home managers should not, if possible, become appointees of residents in their care.

An appointeeship only gives the appointee authority to deal with the resident's benefits and small amounts of capital that have accumulated from these benefits. It does not give any authority to deal with any of the resident's income or capital. In these circumstances, the money has to be administered by the Court of Protection through the Public Guardianship Office.[18]

The Court of Protection[19]

The Court of Protection exists for the protection and management of the property and affairs of persons incapable of managing their own affairs by reason of mental disorder.[20] Any person can apply to the Court to bring another into the Court of Protection, although the implication of Standard 35 is that the applicant should not normally be the manager of the care home. The application must be accompanied by formal medical evidence. Once an order has been made by the Court under this procedure, the Court has exclusive control over the person's property and affairs. It is however common for them to appoint somebody close to the resident to take charge of the management, on a delegated basis. In practice, a considerable number of cases are dealt with more informally by way of a simplified procedure where a resident's estate is less than £16,000, and their financial affairs are reasonably straightforward.[21]

If the Court of Protection or Public Guardianship Office does find the person to be incapable, that person will be referred to as a patient, even though s/he may not be a hospital patient, or detained under the Mental Health Act.

Enduring Power of Attorney[22]

A power of attorney is a legal mechanism where one person (called the donor) can give another person (the attorney) the power to act on their behalf in specified matters. The attorney can enter into legally binding commitments on behalf of the donor. However, this ordinary Power of Attorney comes to an end if the donor becomes mentally incapacitated. In contrast to the ordinary power, an Enduring Power of Attorney can still be valid even if the becomes mentally incapable. Many such arrangements are set up so that they only take effect if and when the donor becomes incapable of managing his/her own affairs due to mental disorder – until this happens, the attorney has no powers. When the donor becomes mentally incapable, the attorney cannot just go ahead and act on the donor's behalf. It is necessary for the attorney to apply to the Court of Protection to register the enduring power. The attorney has to tell the donor and the donor's relatives that such an application is being made, and they can object to it in court. An Enduring Power of Attorney can apply only to the donor's property and affairs, not, for example, to decisions about medical treatment. It will not normally be appropriate for a care home manager to be granted an Enduring Power of Attorney. The Enduring Power of Attorney can be granted to more than one person, to be exercised jointly.

Standard 36

Outcome: Staff are appropriately supervised.

Process: Care staff must receive supervision at least six times a year, to cover all aspects of practice, the philosophy of care in the home, and career development needs. All other staff should be supervised, as part of the normal management process on a continuous basis. Volunteers should also receive training, supervision and support appropriate to their role.

Standard 37

Outcome: Residents' rights and best interests are safeguarded by the home's record keeping policies and procedures.

Process: Residents will have a right of access to their records and any other information about them held by the home, as well as opportunities to help maintain their personal records, which should be secure, up to date and in good order.

Standard 38

Outcome: The health, safety and welfare of residents are promoted and protected.

Process: The care home manager must ensure so far as is reasonably practicable the health, safety and welfare of residents and staff. The registered manager must provide a written statement of the policy, organisation and arrangements for maintaining safe working practices. In addition he/she must ensure that risk assessments are carried out for all safe working practice topics and that significant findings of the risk assessment are recorded.

The registered manager will be expected to ensure compliance with all relevant legislation including:[23]

- Health and Safety at Work Act 1974
- Management of Health and Safety at Work Regulations 1999
- Workplace (Health, Safety and Welfare) Regulations 1992
- Provision and Use of Work Equipment Regulations 1992
- Electricity at Work Regulations 1989
- Health and Safety (First Aid) Regulations 1981
- Control of Substances Hazardous to Health Regulations (COSHH) 1988
- Manual Handling Operations Regulations 1992
- Reporting of Injuries, Diseases and Dangerous Occurrences Regulations (RIDDOR) 1985.

In practical terms this means that the manager must ensure that *safe working practices* are in operation, including:

- *moving and handling*: the use of techniques for moving people and objects that avoid injury to service users or staff;
- *fire safety*: an understanding and implementation of appropriate fire procedures;
- *first aid*: knowledge of how to deal with accidents and health emergencies, provision of a first aid box and a qualified first aider at all times, and recording of all cases reported and handled;
- *food hygiene*: correct storage and preparation of food to avoid food poisoning including labelling and dating of stored food;

- *infection control*: understanding and practice of measures to prevent the spread of infection and communicable diseases.

The manager must further ensure the health and safety of residents and staff through e.g. storage and disposal of hazardous substances, regular servicing of boilers and central heating systems under contract by competent persons (e.g. members of Council of Registered Gas Installers [CORGI]), proper maintenance of electrical systems and electrical equipment, regulation of water temperature, and design solutions to control the risk of Legionella, risks from hot water/surfaces (where temperature is close to 43°C), provision and maintenance of window restrictors, based on assessment of vulnerability of and risk to residents, maintenance of a safe environment, including kitchen equipment and laundry machinery, outdoor steps and pathways, gardening equipment, and security of the premises, and the overall security of the residents based on an assessment of their vulnerability.

All accidents, injuries and incidents of illness or communicable disease must be recorded and reported. Safety procedures must be posted, and explained, in formats that are easily understood and take account of any resident's special communication needs. All staff must receive induction and foundation training and updates to meet TOPSS specification on all safe working practice topics.[24]

ENDNOTES

1   Full text available on http://www.doh.gov.uk/ncsc/carehomes.htm

2   Independent Health Care: National Minimum Standards: Department of Health. Copy of the full text can be obtained at http://www.doh.gov.uk/ncsc/independenthealthcareregs.pdf

3   Letter from Denise Platt, Chief Inspector Social Services CI (2001) 4.

4   See Note on Terminology and Guidance on the Implementation of Regulations and National Minimum Standards, 2002, DoH.

5   This duty to take the standards into account applies to the Commission when making any decision, and in proceedings for urgent cancellations, prosecutions under the Act, and appeals to the Tribunal (s.23 CSA).

6   National Minimum Standards, p.8.

7   The National Care Standards Commission (Registration) Regulations 2001, Regulation 2(1).

8   Defined as 'a short period (normally no longer than six weeks) of intensive rehabilitation and treatment to allow service users to return home following (or to avoid) hospitalisation, or to prevent admission to long term residential care'.

9   Initially, the Commission took the view that a passenger lift could not be a chair or stair lift, but had to be 'a vertical means of transport between floors'. They have now revised this view, so long as what is provided is acceptable, appropriate and meets the needs of the residents. In these circumstances the

provision must take account of any guidance from the Health and Safety Executive and be set out clearly in writing, following the first inspection.

10 When applying this standard, the Commission should take into account their definition of a wheelchair user as 'a person whose main source of independent mobility is a wheelchair'. The standards should not be applied in respect of a resident who is pushed in a wheelchair by staff. It does not require that all doorways are at least 800mm wide but the Commission will need to be satisfied that wheelchair users do not suffer discrimination in the clear access they have to rooms accessible by others.

11 The Commission defines an 'ensuite facility' as 'a room with, at minimum, a toilet and a wash hand basin, which is entered from the service user's bedroom'.

12 Guidance on the Implementation of Regulations and National Minimum Standards issued by the DoH in January 2002 has stated that these room size standards should not be applied until 2007, pointing out that whilst the Commission is entitled to take account of the National Minimum Standards it should always consider individual circumstances when deciding whether it is appropriate to apply them or not. This is probably a pragmatic response to pressure from care home owners, and is a sensible approach.

13 This provision in the Standards has caused much controversy as many care homes traditionally rely upon assistants under 18 to help with personal care. The position of the Commission is that 'service users consulted in the preparation of the national minimum standards indicated that they did not like to have their personal care needs met by very young staff i.e. children/young people aged under 18'. www.doh.gov.uk/ncsc/qandaregs.htm

14 See also Standard 38, p.72.

15 Any agency staff working in the home are included in the 50 per cent ratio.

16 See www.doh.gov.uk/gscc

17 pp. 131–5.

18 For more information contact Public Guardianship Office, Archway Tower, 2 Junction Road, London N19 5RQ or consult website at www.guardianship.gov.uk

19 For more detail see The Court of Protection Rules 2001 SI 2001 No. 824 and The Court of Protection (Amendment) Rules 2001 SI 2001 No. 2977, or consult P. Letts (1998) *Managing Other People's Money*. London: Age Concern.

20 s.93 Mental Health Act 1983.

21 See generally *Elderly Client Adviser* Vol 7(1) 2001, 3–4. The Court's personal application branch is Stewart House, 24 Kingsway, London WC2B 6JX.

22 The procedures relating to the registration of an Enduring Power of Attorney and the objections that can be made to registration are set out in the Court of Protection (Enduring Power of Attorney) Rules 2001, SI 2001, No 825. For further information, contact the Public Guardianship Office, above at Note 18.

23 For a basic outline of the main provisions see the NCHA booklet *Health and Safety in Residential and Nursing Homes at Work*, or for a more substantial account, see *Health and Safety in Care Homes*, 2001, Health and Safety Executive, HSG 220.

24 See Chapter Nine at p.131.

CHAPTER FIVE

What is the Role of Local Authorities in the Provision of Residential Accommodation?

THE DUTY TO ASSESS

Residential accommodation forms part of the 'community care services' provided by each local authority. By virtue of the National Health Service and Community Care Act 1990, s.47:[1]

> Each local authority is obliged by law (regardless of its available resources) to carry out an assessment of any person ordinarily resident in its area, who appears to be in need of any of its community care services (which include, in certain defined circumstances, residential accommodation).[2]

The framework within which all local authorities should determine eligibility for their adult care services is set out in DoH LASSA guidance 'Fair access to care services'[3] supplemented by the general principles of assessment.[4] The aim of this guidance is to provide social services with a framework for determining eligibility for adult care services that has hitherto been absent. Assessments will grade people into four bands, based on the seriousness of the risk to independence if the problems and isssues disclosed are not addressed. Under the draft framework guidance, local authorities must review their eligibility criteria at least annually, and should carry out an initial review of their first assessment after three months, and at least annually thereafter.

Since April 2002, the assessment forms a part of the Single Assessment Process (SAP) outlined by the Government in the National Service Framework for Older People. Guidance on the operation of the SAP has been issued as s.7 LASSA guidance.[5]

The purpose of assessment is 'to describe and evaluate individuals' problems and issues and the attendant impact on independence in the immediate and longer term'.[6] Assessment should be carried out in such a way as to be sufficiently transparent for individuals to:[7]

- gain a better understanding of their situation;
- identify the options that are available for managing their own lives;
- understand the basis on which decisions are reached.

The SAP recognises that many older people have health and social care needs and that:

> Agencies need to work together so that assessment and subsequent planning are person-centred, effective and co-ordinated. [SAP] will ensure that the scale and depth of assessment is kept in proportion to older people's needs, that agencies do not duplicate each other's assessments and that professionals contribute to assessments in the most effective way.[8]

SAP is not however intended to be a single assessment tool; rather it provides a framework that will lead to a convergence of assessment methods into a common single, pooled statement of the applicant's need. The SAP is used in the determination of level of nursing care required by a resident, in line with the Registered Nursing Care Contribution (RNCC) (see pp.87–90). In addition it should be noted that[9] a registered person must not provide accommodation at the care home unless, so far as it shall have been practicable to do so, the needs of the person seeking accommodation have been assessed by a suitably qualified or suitably trained person and:

1. the assessed person has obtained a copy of the assessment;

2. there has been appropriate consultation regarding the assessment with that person, or his/her representative;

3. the registered person has confirmed in writing to the resident that having regard to the assessment, the care home is suitable for the purpose of meeting his/her needs in respect of health and welfare. It should also be recorded whether or not the service user has agreed to the plan, or the reason why this was not possible.

The registered person must also ensure that the assessment of the resident's needs is kept under review, and in any event is reviewed at any time when it is necessary to do so, having regard to any change of circumstances.

WHAT ARE THE LOCAL AUTHORITY'S RESPONSIBILITIES FOLLOWING ASSESSMENT?

Having carried out an assessment, local authority social services departments are under a duty to provide residential accommodation for people who satisfy *both* the following two tests:[10]

Test One

The person must be *either*:

1. ordinarily resident in the area of the local authority; *or*

2. in that area with no settled residence anywhere; *or*

3. ordinarily resident elsewhere but nevertheless in the area at the time of application *and in urgent need of residential care.*[11]

In addition, the local authority can offer accommodation to any other persons provided that the local authority in whose area they normally reside consents. The phrase 'ordinarily resident' requires the person to show a regular, habitual mode of life in a particular place, the continuity of which has persisted, despite temporary absences (*Shah v Barnet LBC* (1983)):[12]

> Ordinary residence is to be given its ordinary and natural meaning…i.e. a (person's) abode in a particular place or country which [he/she] has adopted voluntarily and for settled purposes as part of the regular order of [his/her] life for the time being, whether of short or long duration. (Per Lord Scarman)

Note that Circular LAC (93) 9 para. 12 advises that except in cases involving persons with severe learning disabilities, adults with learning disabilities should be regarded as capable of forming their own intention of where they wish to live. (If two or more social services departments are in dispute over a person's ordinary residence the NAA 1948 s.32(3) and LAC (93)7 lay down a detailed procedure for resolving the dispute.)

Test Two

The person must be aged 18 or over and, by reason of age, illness, disability or any other circumstance in need of care and attention not otherwise available to him/her (s.21(1)(a) NAA) *or* an expectant or nursing mother who is in need of care and attention which is not otherwise available to her.

A number of these terms require clarification:

- *Age.* This is usually taken as reference to the frail elderly, and also includes elderly mentally infirm people.[13] Note that is not linked to any *specific* age.

- *Illness.* This is not defined by the Act. Note that the Secretary of State's Direction 1993 has recommended that care and attention may be required, not merely because the person is ill, but in order to prevent that person becoming ill, or by way of after-care.[14]

- *Disability.* Unlike the definition of 'disability' for the purposes of CSDPA[15] services, it is *not* necessary for the disability to be 'substantial and permanent' for the purposes of these services.

- *Any other circumstance.* The Secretary of State's Direction 1993[16] specifically includes two categories of condition under this description, but this does not exclude the possibility of other conditions being included. The two categories are:

  1. *Mental disorder,* including for the prevention of mental disorder, and for after-care purposes. This includes those with no settled residence, who are nevertheless in the local authority's area.

  2. *Alcohol or drug dependency,* limited to dependency, rather than prevention.

- *Care and attention.* As this phrase is also not defined it should be given a literal, subjective interpretation and be interpreted as widely as possible, but in a common sense way. The courts have frequently stressed that a person can be in need of care and attention simply by virtue of being destitute. See *R. v Hammersmith and Fulham LBC ex p. M* (1997):[17]

  > The whole purpose of the National Assistance Act 1948 was to en-sure that no-one would be left destitute because of an inability to fend for himself. It seems to me that in ordinary English usage someone who is unable to provide for himself the basic necessities of life can properly be said to be in need of care and attention. (Per Collins J.)

- *Not otherwise available to them.* As the philosophy of the community care approach is to emphasise the desirability of care in the community at large, it is important that residential care is seen as a last resort, and that all other avenues are excluded before this route is adopted, including any entitlements under the Housing

Act 1996 or a domiciliary care package. It should be noted that care and attention is not to be regarded as 'otherwise available' to an applicant, if they cannot afford to pay for it (*R v Sefton MBC ex p. Help the Aged* (1997).[18] This provision has been specifically clarified in the Community Care (Residential Accommodation) Act 1998, s.1 as follows:

> For the purposes of deciding whether care and attention is *otherwise available to the person*, a local authority shall disregard so much of the person's capital as does not exceed the current capital limit (£18,500) for these purposes, i.e. capital below this figure should be ignored as a potential alternative means for funding the person's care and attention needs.

Even if the person's capital does exceed £18,500, the local authority may still decide that care and attention is not otherwise available to that person, for example if s/he lacks mental capacity.

THE SPECIAL RULES FOR PERSONS 'SUBJECT TO IMMIGRATION CONTROL'.

Section 21 'residential accommodation'[19] will not be provided to persons who are destitute, but 'subject to immigration control',[20] if their 'need of care and attention' has arisen solely because they are 'destitute' or because of the physical effects, or anticipated physical effects of being 'destitute'. The word 'destitute' is defined for these purposes as follows:

> The person does not have adequate accommodation or the means of obtaining it, *or* the person has adequate accommodation, or the means of obtaining it, but cannot meet their essential living requirements.[21]

Note however that the important case of *R v Wandsworth LBC ex p. O* (2000)[22] has decided that where the needs of destitute people for care and attention are to any material extent made more acute by some circumstance other than mere lack of accommodation and funds (for example, age, illness or disability) then notwithstanding the fact that they are 'subject to immigration control', they will qualify for assistance.

> If there are to be immigrant beggars on our streets, then let them at least not be old, ill or disabled. (Per Lord Justice Simon Brown)

> Social workers are not professionals in making moral judgements as between different people with identical needs. They have no particular skills or facilities for assessing whether or not a person is subject to immigration control or

has a real choice about whether or not to return to his (or her) home country. (Per Lady Justice Hale)

If the applicant is also in the category of 'asylum seeker',[23] s/he falls within the protection of NASS, the National Asylum Support Scheme, which was set up in 1999 to support 'asylum seekers' who were otherwise destitute.

> Social Services Departments should not carry the burden of looking after healthy and able-bodied asylum-seekers. This task will fall to the [NASS]. (White Paper, July 1999)

Under this scheme,[24] the Home Secretary is empowered to disperse asylum seekers across the country, and to compel local authority landlords to participate in the provision of accommodation for them, subject to financial compensation from central government. However, the case of *R on the Application of Westminster City Council v NASS* (2001),[25] has decided that where an asylum seeker has a need for care and attention, 'which does not arise solely from either destitution, or its physical or anticipated physical effects' (in this case, a serious medical condition, spinal myeloma, needing constant medical care, and unconnected with destitution), the local authority are *not* relieved of their duties to supply the applicant with residential accommodation, and they should not therefore refer the case to NASS in these circumstances.[26]

WHAT HAPPENS FOLLOWING ASSESSMENT?

If, following the above assessment procedures and criteria, the local authority decides the applicant is in need of residential accommodation, they are obliged to make arrangements for accommodating that person. This responsibility rests with the local authority as a whole. Thus, even though the housing department would not treat the case as a priority under its own internal guidelines, priority provision must be made if a s.21 assessment by the social services department has concluded it is necessary, as set out above. In the case of *R v Islington LBC ex p. Batantu* (2000),[27] the social services department carried out a community care assessment on a large family, in which the father suffered from severe mental health problems. They decided that the family needed a ground floor property, with a large amount of safe, secure and easily accessible space. They believed that the father's severe mental health problems were being exacerbated by the family's current accommodation, from which they sought to transfer. The housing department's view was different, but deemed by the Court to be an irrelevance, as the community care needs assessment was the determining factor.

CAN A LOCAL AUTHORITY TAKE ITS OWN RESOURCES INTO ACCOUNT WHEN DECIDING WHETHER IT MUST PROVIDE RESIDENTIAL ACCOMMODATION TO APPLICANTS?

The Court of Appeal determined in 1997 that there was a 'limited subjective element' in making an assessment, as to whether a person has a 'need for care and attention', which means that a local authority may have regard to its limited financial resources in deciding whether an applicant seeking residential accommodation is 'in need of care and attention'. Once a decision has been made, however, that a person *is* 'in need of care and attention which is not otherwise available to them', a *duty* arises to make arrangements to provide appropriate residential accommodation, which duty cannot be avoided by a claim of lack of resources (*R. v Sefton MBC ex p. Help the Aged* (1997).[28]

Also in this case the Court decided that 'care and attention is not to be regarded as otherwise available if the person concerned is unable to pay for it according to the means test regime provided for'.[29]

CAN THE APPLICANT BE PUT ON A WAITING LIST UNTIL SUITABLE ACCOMMODATION OR FUNDING BECOMES AVAILABLE?

A recent Scots case, *R v South Lanarkshire Council ex p. MacGregor* (2001),[30] has decided that once a person has been assessed under the above procedures, as being in need of residential care, it will be unlawful for the local authority to do nothing to resolve the need to find suitable accommodation, on the basis of a short-term lack of resources.

> Having decided that [the applicant] was unable to care for himself and that he had insufficient funds to pay for residential care, the local authority was under a duty to make some provision for his care. The nature of that care is a matter for the local authority but the decision to do nothing and place him on a waiting list is in my opinion *ultra vires*.

Although Scots law is not strictly binding on English law, the framework of the relevant Scots legislation is the National Assistance Act 1948. In addition the wording of the relevant English law[31] places an even stronger duty on the English and Welsh local authorities. Thus it seems fair to say that the case is now a good statement of the legal position across the whole of Great Britain.

FINDING THE RIGHT HOME

Note that all of the above responsibilities and definitions refer to the phrase 'residential accommodation'.

What is residential accommodation?

In the case of *R. v Newham LBC ex p. Medical Foundation* (1997)[32] the Court held that:

> Residential accommodation is a place where a person lives, normally with a degree of permanence. It need not have any institutional quality [and] can as a matter of law be accommodation at which there is no provision of board or other services, no nursing care and no personal care.

Residential accommodation for older people in care homes is provided from three different sectors: local authorities, voluntary (non-profit-making) organisations and the private sector. Although the sources of funding of each category of home will clearly differ, there is considerable overlap in practice between the three sectors, with each sector being subject to statutory regulation, and many older people being placed by local authorities in one of the other two sectors, either because there is no available space in any local authority home, or because the home in question is more suitable to the needs and wishes of the older person. If a person is homeless or threatened with homelessness the local authority housing department should be contacted in the first instance. Most housing departments have special units for dealing with applications from homeless people. In all other cases, responsibility with regard to residential accommodation rests with the social services department. The local authority should normally offer applicants a particular home, or choice of homes. However, if applicants do not like the home offered, or wish to be given a place in an alternative home, they have a right to request such an alternative, which the local authority must provide, so long as:

- the accommodation is suitable to the person's assessed needs; and
- a place is available; and
- the accommodation in question is willing to enter into a contract on the authority's usual terms and conditions; and
- the accommodation does not cost more than the authority would usually expect to pay for someone with similar needs.

The High Court has stressed the importance of this last point, stating that where the needs assessment is clear about the type of home necessary to meet the applicant's particular needs, it is not open to the local authority to offer accommodation that does not meet the fully assessed needs (including their psychological needs) simply on the grounds that it is cheaper (*R v Avon CC ex p. M* (1999)).[33] In the recent case of *R v Richmond LBC ex p. T* (2000),[34] a local authority offered an applicant who had a history of mental health problems accommodation in a block of flats, which his doctor maintained was 'not suitable to his mental health needs'. The Court ordered the local authority:

> To provide the applicant with his lawfully assessed needs, including his psychological needs within three months.

Furthermore, if an applicant with mental health problems refuses to accept the accommodation offered, and the local authority considers this to be an unreasonable refusal, the authority cannot discharge its responsibility to that applicant until it can show that it explained to the applicant the consequences of such refusal 'to the point of comprehension' (*R v Newham LBC ex p. P* (2000)).[35]

If a third party is willing and able to pay the additional costs of a more expensive home, the local authority is obliged to accept this offer and to arrange a place in the more expensive home, recouping the difference from the third party. It is increasingly the case that people are choosing a home in an area outside that of the authority that has assessed their needs, for example an area where their close relatives live. In these circumstances, the local authority in which the applicant is normally resident, and which has therefore carried out the assessment, will still be obliged to pay for the accommodation (subject to the normal means test, but only up to the level of their own standard rate[36]).

WHO PAYS FOR THE ACCOMMODATION?

If, following a community care assessment, a local authority agrees to arrange a place for the applicant in residential accommodation, the local authority will be responsible for paying the full fee to the home. VAT is not charged on home care fees. In 1999, publicly funded care accounted for around 70 per cent of the take-up of places in care and nursing homes.[37] The great majority of this funding was provided by local authorities.[38] Having paid the fees directly to the home, the local authority can then try to recoup all or some of the fees from the applicant under the charging assessment procedures. This procedure applies regardless of the type of accommodation (i.e. council, voluntary or private). It is of course always possible to arrange residential care accommodation without recourse to any local authority assistance in the matter. If a person has not gone through the assessment procedures outlined above, however, he/she will be responsible for his/her own fees. If at a later stage, however, s/he finds s/he is no longer able to afford the fees, s/he can approach the local authority in the area where s/he is now living. The local authority will assess his/her needs 'as soon as is reasonably practicable' and if necessary take over the financial arrangements so that the resident is not forced to use up capital below the limit.[39]

WHAT ARE THE CHARGING ASSESSMENT PROCEDURES?

The local authority must set a standard rate (a weekly charge) for the accommodation, which in the case of its own accommodation is the full cost of providing a place, and in the case of other homes (whether private or voluntary homes) is the gross cost of paying for the accommodation, under the contract with the home. The rate must not however include the costs of any 'nursing care' that is to be provided to the resident (see p.95). In 2001, the average weekly charge rates in pounds sterling across the United Kingdom were as follows (figures are based upon a singe room occupancy):

Residential homes

	Private	Voluntary
SE	274	301
East Anglia	250	271
SW	232	236
West Midlands	245	250
East Midlands	234	233
NW	232	239
NE	230	243
N	232	244
Wales	228	236
Scotland	261	288
NI	229	227
Weighted Average	**247**	**267**

Nursing homes

	Private	Voluntary
SE	406	407
East Anglia	320	399
SW	339	322
West Midlands	325	337
East Midlands	298	296
NW	306	311
NE	295	284
N	275	329
Wales	284	283
Scotland	338	336
NI	301	292
Weighted Average	**335**	**350**

Figure 5.1 Average weekly charge rates (in pounds sterling) for residential accommodation

The charging assessment procedure is carried out according to national rules. The procedure is normally applied to 'prospective' residents, prior to their being placed in residential accommodation, taking into account any capital or other resources they have at that time.[40]

The rules resemble those used for determining income support, and take into the account both capital and income. The local authority will apply a 'means test' to the resident, in order to determine how much, if any, of the standard rate will be charged to the resident.

Every resident must be allowed to retain a weekly minimum personal allowance.[41] In 2001 this figure was £16.05 per week. The local authority does have a discretion to allow residents to keep more than this statutory minimum, to enable them to lead more independent lives.[42] Guidance[43] suggests that where residents are temporarily absent from the home, for example staying with friends or relatives, or where they need to help support their partner at home, these are circumstances when the personal expenses allowance might legitimately be raised.

Capital includes all the applicant's savings, investments and the value of the applicant's home, unless his/her spouse, unmarried partner, a relative aged 60 or over, a relative under 60 who is incapacitated, or a child under 16 whom the resident has a responsibility to maintain continues to live there. The value of the home is also ignored:[44]

- so long as the stay in the residential accommodation remains temporary (i.e. unlikely to exceed 52 weeks); and

- thereafter, for the first 12 weeks that the stay is permanent.

Where the value of a home is taken into account the value is based upon the current market value less any charges secured against it (e.g. a mortgage), less a further 10 per cent in recognition of the fees incurred in an eventual sale. Once the house is sold, the actual capital remaining post-sale is the figure used.

Capital between £11,500 and £18,500 is deemed to generate £1 income per £250. Capital below £11,500 is ignored, but where the applicant's assessed capital exceeds £18,500, s/he will not be entitled to receive any financial assistance from the local authority in respect of the payment of residential home fees. Applicants with more than £18,500 in savings may be deemed to have 'access to alternative care and attention' by virtue of their capital.[45] If they are, nevertheless, accommodated by the local authority they will be asked to pay the full 'standard rate', as a 'self-funder'. It is the view of the DoH, however, that having capital in excess of £18,500 does not *in itself* constitute adequate access to alternative care and attention:

Local authorities must satisfy themselves that the individual is able to make their own arrangements, or has others who are willing and able to make arrangements for them, for appropriate care.[46]

If a 'self-funder'[47] enters a nursing home, and his/her capital is reduced below the £18,500 upper capital limit, it is the view of the DoH that:

The local authority should undertake an assessment as soon as is reasonably practicable, and if necessary step in to take over arrangements so as to ensure the resident is not forced to use up capital, below [£18,500].[48]

CAN APPLICANTS TRANSFER THEIR ASSETS TO THEIR FAMILY PRIOR TO MOVING INTO RESIDENTIAL ACCOMMODATION?

As stated above, if the applicant owns his/her own home, this will be treated as capital, unless to do so would cause hardship to somebody with whom s/he had previously been sharing the home on a long-term basis. It is not possible for those who anticipate going into residential accommodation to avoid this charge on their capital by transferring their house to someone else shortly before moving into the residential accommodation. Regulation 25 of the National Assistance (Assessment of Resources) Regulations 1992[49] specifically states:

A resident may be treated as possessing actual capital of which s/he has deprived him/herself for the purpose of decreasing the amount that s/he may be liable to pay for his accommodation.

The law allows a local authority to recover payment from anyone to whom a person in residential accommodation has transferred assets (including a house) less than six months before entering residential accommodation if it can be shown that they did so 'knowingly and with the intention of avoiding charges for the residential accommodation'. If it can be shown, on the balance of probabilities, that the transfer was manifestly to avoid payment, recovery can in fact be enforced even if the transfer was more than six months prior to entering accommodation (Housing and Social Services and Social Security Adjudications Act 1983 (HSSSSAA)). Furthermore, it is not necessary for the local authority in these circumstances to prove that the claimant knew of the existence of the capital limits and had foreseen an application for funding for residential accommodation being made.

The true purpose of any transfer may be ascertained or inferred from the material provided by the resident and those advising them without any specific finding as to the state of knowledge or intention of the resident. See

Yule v South Lanarkshire Council [50], where an elderly woman transferred her property to a favourite granddaughter 'in consideration of love, favour and affection' retaining a life rent, and the court concluded that the council were entitled to form the view that the motive for the disposition was avoidance of the full cost of future residential accommodation fees.

In the case of *R on the Application of the Personal Representative of Christopher Beeson v Dorset Council* (2001) [51] the High Court did however stress that the test of intent and purpose is always a subjective test. A father had transferred his property to his son, two years before his death with no subjective belief that he would ever have to enter a care home. The High Court decided that the local authority could not conclude that the intent and purpose of the transaction was to transfer assets that would otherwise be available to pay for care home accommodation. The case also ruled that the Council's failure to provide the applicant with an independent and impartial appeals procedure against their original decision, to treat this transaction as an intent to transfer assets, breached Article 6 of the European Convention on Human Rights, and was therefore unlawful, although this decision was subsequently modified by the Court of Appeal.

Whilst a local authority cannot force a person to sell his/her home in order to meet the standard charge that it wishes to levy, it can protect its financial interest by paying the fees direct to the home, and placing a legal charge on the property, to cover the cost of the fees at a later stage. This legal charge will entitle them to recover the fees, when the property is ultimately transferred either by will, or on intestacy or sale.

Since October 2001, local authorities have been able to claim compensation from the government if they put a charge on the property but do not require its immediate sale. This procedure is known as the deferred payments scheme. It is available to care home residents who have less than £18, 500 capital (disregarding the value of their home) and insufficient income to meet the cost of the care home fees. [52] In these circumstances the resident will be treated, to all intents and purposes, as a person paying his/her own fees, with the actual payment being suspended until such time as the property is sold. [53] In the meantime, the local authority will pay the full fees to the home. A resident in this situation can however claim the care component of disability living allowance or attendance allowance, so long as s/he is not in receipt of income support or housing benefit. [54]

In addition to placing a charge on the resident's house to protect the local authority's financial position in the event of non-payment of the fees, the local authority can also issue proceedings in any court for the recovery of any outstanding debts, or proceedings against the resident's spouse, but not against any other member of his/her family.

The pre-1993 group

People already in residential care or nursing homes on 31 March 1993 had 'preserved rights', and the above charging rules have not therefore historically applied to them. The distinction between the two types of resident ceased from April 2002. Local authorities are now responsible for the assessment, care management and financial support of this group of residents. Regulations and LASSA guidance have been issued setting out the details of the new arrangements.[55]

ENDNOTES

1   Available online at http://www.hmso.gov.uk/acts/acts1990/Ukpga_19900019_en_1.htm

2   This term is not limited to the provision of accommodation in a residential care or nursing home. The term 'residential' means simply 'accommodation where a person lives'. The key case is *R v Newham LBC ex p. Medical Foundation* (1998) 1 CCLR 227, in which the court held as follows:

> Residential accommodation is a place where a person lives, normally with a degree of permanence. It need not have any institutional quality and can as a matter of law be accommodation at which there is no provision of board or other services.

3   *Fair Access to Care Services,* DoH 2002.

4   *General Principles of Assessment for Adult Social Care,* DoH 2002.

5   For significance of this term, see Note on Terminology.

6   *General Principles of Assessment for Adult Social Care: Policy Guidance Consultation Draft,* July 2001, DoH, para. 6.

7   *General Principles of Assessment for Adult Social Care: Policy Guidance Consultation Draft,* July 2001, DoH, para. 6.

8   *The Single Assessment Process, Guidance for Local Implementation, Consultation Draft,* July 2001, DoH, para.6.

9   Care Homes Regulation 14.

10   This duty arises from a combination of s. 21 National Assistance Act 1948 and the Secretary of State's Direction 1993 LAC (93) 10.

11   National Assistance Act 1948, s.24.

12   (1983) 1 All ER 226.

13   See Clements, L. in *Community Care and the Law,* Legal Action Group, 2000, at 4.11.

14   LAC (93) 10 Appendix 1 para. 2(5).

15   Chronically Sick and Disabled Persons Act 1970. See generally Clements, L. (2000) *Community Care and the Law* (2nd Edition). Legal Action Group.

16   LAC (93) 10 Appendix 1 para. 2(5).

17   (1997) 1 CCLR 69.

18   (1997) 1 CCLR 57.

19   See p.82.

20   s.115 of the Immigration and Asylum Act 1999: 'A person who is not a national of an EEA state and who EITHER requires leave to enter or remain in the UK but does not have it; OR has leave to enter or remain in the UK, which is subject to a condition that he or she does not have recourse to public funds or following a maintenance undertaking; OR has leave to enter or remain in the UK given as a result of a maintenance undertaking, OR who is appealing against a decision to vary or refuse to vary limited leave.'

21   s.95 (3) Immigration and Asylum Act 1999.

22   (2000) 3 CCLR 237.

23   Defined by s.94(1) of the Immigration and Asylum Act 1999 as 'a person who has made a claim for asylum which has been recorded by the Secretary of State but which has not been determined'.

24   More information about NASS can be found at www.ind.homeoffice.gov.uk

25   (2001) 4 CCLR 143 subsequently upheld in the Court of Appeal.

26   See also *O v Wandsworth LBC* (2000) 3 CCLR 237.

27   2000 *Legal Action* January 2001, 28.

28   (1997) 1 CCLR 57. See also *R v Wigan MBC ex p. Tammadge* (1998) 1 CCLR 581, which established that it was unlawful for a meeting attended by councillors to override the decision on need of the council's own professionally qualified staff and advisers.

29   See above at pp.78–9 under 'Not otherwise available to them', for further clarification of this point.

30   (2001) 4 CCLR 188.

31   s.21 National Assistance Act 1948.

32   (1998) 1 CCLR 69.

33   (1999) 2 CCLR 185.

34   2000 *Legal Action*, January 2001, 28.

35   2000 *Legal Action*, January 2001, 28.

36   See below, 'What are the charging assessment procedures?'.

37   *Laing's Healthcare Market Review 1999–2000*, Laing and Buisson, December 1999.

38   *Association of Directors of Social Services: National Minimum Standards – Single/Shared Room Ratio*, ADSS 2000.

39   LGOR 99/C/0619 Cumbria.

40   The detailed procedures and rules of the means test are set out in The National Assistance (Assessment of Resources) Regulation 1992 http://www.legislation.hmso.gov.uk/si/ si1992/Uksi_19922977_en_1.htm and the DoH 'guidance' *The Charging for Residential Accommodation Guide* (CRAG), available free of charge from DOH@prologistics.co.uk (updated regularly).

41   The amount of the allowance is determined annually by Parliament. For latest figures see National Assistance (Sums for Personal Expenses) Regulations 2000. http://www.legislation.hmso.gov.uk/si/si2000/20000798.htm

42   National Assistance Act 1948 s.22(4).

43   LAC 97/5, Annex H, CRAG.

44   For further guidance on these provisions see LAC (2001) 25.

45   See pp.78–9.

46   LASSA Circular Guidance, the Community Care (Residential Accommodation) Act 1998, LAC (98) 19.

47   This term includes those whose income is supplemented by certain state benefits such as Disability Living Allowance.

48   LASSA Circular Guidance, Community Care (Residential Accommodation) Act 1998, LAC (98) 19.

49   Available online at http://www.legislation.hmso.gov.uk/si/si1992/Uksi_19922977_en_1.htm

50   (1999) 2 CCLR 394.

51   Case No: CO/2512001.

52   See LAC (2001) 25.

53   Social Security Commissioner Decision CA/2937/1997.

54   Disability Rights Handbook, 26th Edition, p.174.

55   The Preserved Rights (Transfer of Responsibilities to Local Authorities) Regulations 2001; (Draft) Guidance to Councils with Social Services Responsibilities on the Abolition of Preserved Rights, issued October 2001. (Final version due to be published in early March.)

CHAPTER SIX

The Provision of Nursing Care

The National Minimum Standards form the core of the new regime for the regulation of the quality of provision in care homes. The standards that cover nursing care are Standards 7–11. Whilst the National Minimum Standards are not law, they provide the benchmarks against which the registration and inspection systems operate.[1]

The care plan that is required to be drawn up for every care home resident (see Standard 7 below) must include details of any nursing care that is also to be provided to the resident. It must be shown that the care plan, so far as it is practicable, enables residents to make decisions with respect to the care they are to receive and their health and welfare, by ascertaining and taking into account their wishes and feelings.[2] Any nursing care[3] to be provided as part of the care plan will be provided using the Registered Nursing Care Contribution method (RNCC).[4] The Nursing Home Fees Agency (NHFA) has published a long-term care guide, together with a series of information sheets providing useful information on these issues.[5]

HEALTH AND PERSONAL CARE: 7–11

Standard 7

Outcome: The resident's health, personal and social care will be set out in an individual plan of care.

Process: The care plan derived from Standard 3[6] must set out in detail the action that needs to be taken by care staff to ensure that 'all aspects of the health, personal and social care needs of the resident are met'. The plan must meet relevant clinical guidelines, including a risk assessment, and must be reviewed by the care staff in the home at least once a month. The drawing up of the plan must involve the resident, and the resident must agree to and sign it, if capable of doing so.

Standard 8

Outcome: The resident's health care needs will be fully met.

Process: The care home must be able to demonstrate that it provides either directly, or through access to third parties, the full range of appropriate health care services capable of meeting the needs established in the care plan.

Standard 9

Outcome: Residents, where appropriate, are responsible for their own medication, and will be protected by the home's policies and procedures for dealing with medicines.

Process: To satisfy this standard the person responsible for the care home must ensure that there is in place a clear and effective set of procedures for the receipt, recording, storage, handling, administration and disposal of medicines, and that residents are able to take responsibility for their own medication, if they so wish, within a risk management framework. In addition, staff must monitor the conditions of the resident on medication, and liaise with the GP if concerns arise. When a service user dies, medicines must be retained for a period of seven days, in case there is a coroner's inquest.

Standard 10

Outcome: Residents will feel they are treated with respect and their right to privacy upheld.

Process: To satisfy this outcome, the home must adopt an overall approach ensuring that its residents experience a sense of privacy and dignity at all times. Particular sensitivity should be observed in entering bedrooms, toilets and bathrooms if a resident is present, in personal care-giving, when residents are in consultation with health and social care professionals, or with legal or financial advisers, when they are maintaining social contacts with relatives and friends, and following a death.

Standard 11

Outcome: Residents will be assured that at the time of their death, staff will treat them and their family with care, sensitivity and respect.

Process: The care home must demonstrate that they will give special care and comfort to residents who are dying, and that their deaths will be handled with dignity and propriety, and their spiritual needs, and associated rites and functions, will be observed.

NURSING CARE

In many but not all care homes, nursing care is available to residents who require it as part of the overall service for residents. Since October 2001, no self-funding care home resident, following an assessment of need, should be charged for any nursing care they require from a registered nurse in a care home. The funding of such nursing care has become the responsibility of the 'relevant NHS body', which will be either the health authority or a care trust.[7] From April 2003 the NHS will also become responsible for paying for the nursing care of residents supported by their local authorities, and local authorities will be expressly prohibited from providing, or arranging to provide, nursing services.[8] Although the Health Act 1999 allows NHS bodies and local authorities to enter into collaborative arrangements in relation to the exercise of some of their functions, the Act makes it clear that:[9]

> Any such collaborative working together will not affect the legal liability of either body for the proper exercise of their legal duties, nor the power or the duty of a local authority to recover their charges.

Care homes should automatically receive a payment from the NHS in respect of nursing care received by each resident, at the appropriate band. The amount of money provided to the care home to cover the cost of its nursing care is described as the Registered Nursing Care Contribution (RNCC). In theory, care home residents in receipt of nursing care should see a consequential reduction in their fees to reflect this increased NHS input into the home, via the RNCC.

MANAGEMENT AND ADMINISTRATION OF NURSING CARE ASSESSMENT/RNCC PROCESS

The management and administration of the assessment process and determination of support bandings for nursing care provision is the responsibility of the nursing home co-ordinator, who is the lead manager for free nursing care within the health authority (HA) or primary care trust (PCT) responsible for the nursing care. S/he is also the budget holder for these funds. The responsibilities of the nursing home co-ordinator are as follows:

1. To manage, on behalf of the NHS, the budget for NHS-funded nursing care, including the responsibility for agreement that this budget will fund each individual's nursing care, and day-to-day budget management.

2. To monitor spending on nursing care against the allocated budget, and to ensure that spend stays within budget.

3. To liaise with local nursing homes, identifying eligible residents.

4. To liaise with social service contacts on the provision of services and the identification of eligible residents.

5. To liaise closely with nurses carrying out determinations of care by a registered nurse for existing and future nursing home residents, approving the funding of all nursing determinations that are carried out by nurses.

6. To manage, in conjunction with nurses, the reviews of determinations of care by a registered nurse, including any formal reviews that might need to be referred to the continuing care panel.

7. To act as the lead manager for NHS-funded nursing care within the HA/PCT.

8. To liaise with HAs/PCTs and local councils on placements[10] 'in local nursing homes out of area'.[11]

9. To act as a focal point for any complaints about NHS-funded nursing care in so far as these might relate to the provision of NHS services, and as a channel for complaints elsewhere (in the HA, councils with social service responsibilities, Ombudsman, etc.) as necessary.

The HA/PCT must also appoint a second manager, known as the lead nurse for free nursing care, who will work in conjunction with the co-ordinator, and whose responsibilities will be as follows:

1.   To provide professional nursing advice to nursing homes, councils and the nursing home co-ordinator about the carrying out of determinations and use of the Registered Nursing Care Contribution (RNCC).

2.   To monitor the quality and consistency of nursing determinations of care by a registered nurse carried out within the HA/PCT.

3.   To ensure that a sufficient number of nurses, as set out in the related guidance on the use of the RNCC, receive appropriate training in the use of the RNCC.

SOME KEY DEFINITIONS

Nursing Care

'Nursing care' is defined, in the context of care homes, as:

> Any services provided by a registered nurse and involving either a) the provision of care or b) the planning, supervision, or delegation of care, other than any services which do not need to be provided by a registered nurse.[12]

A 'registered nurse' means a nurse registered by the Nursing and Midwifery Council, with a qualification in nursing, midwifery or health visiting recognised by the Council. Nursing care does not therefore extend to any nursing services provided by health care assistants, which services will therefore continue to be liable to a charge, subject to a means test.

In addition, any self-funding individuals who wish to continue paying for their nursing themselves, and do not wish to receive NHS funding, are at liberty to do so, by notifying the nursing home co-ordinator that this is their wish.

The amount of funding provided for an individual's nursing care will be determined by an assessment,[13] to establish the level of the RNCC. This determination will place the level of nursing care to be provided, in one of three bandings.[14] It is proposed that these bandings will be reviewed after 12 months' operation of the scheme with a view to revising the bands, to come into effect from 2003/4.[15] The bands are national and there can be no variation in the amounts paid across the country.

Low Band: This will apply to people whose care needs can be met with minimal registered nurse input. Assessment will indicate that these needs could normally be met in another setting (such as at home by a district nurse), but the person has chosen to place him/herself in a nursing home (£35 per week).

Medium Band: This will apply to people having multiple care needs, requiring the intervention of a registered nurse on at least a daily basis, and maybe needing access to a nurse at any time. Their condition (including physical, behavioural and psycho-social needs) will nevertheless be stable and predictable, and likely to remain so, if the treatment and care regimes continue (£70 per week).

High Band: This will apply to people with complex nursing needs that require frequent mechanical, technical and/or therapeutic interventions, throughout a 24-hour period. In addition, their physical or mental state will be unstable and/or unpredictable (£110 per week).

Where an individual already has a package of continuing health and social care provided by NHS and social services and his/her needs have not changed, the use of the RNCC should not decrease the NHS's contribution to the person's care.

Continuing NHS health care

Note that health authorities also provide continuing NHS health care, over and above the 'nursing care' outlined above. This is defined as 'a package of care arranged, and funded solely by, the NHS. It does not include the provision by local councils of any social services.'[16] Where an individual's primary need is health care, then the whole package of care must be paid for by the NHS. People receiving continuing NHS health care can be placed in a hospital or a care home, or they can receive the NHS health care in their own homes, with the NHS meeting the full cost of their health care needs.[17] Nothing in the RNCC procedures changes the continuing responsibilities of health authorities to arrange and fully fund services for people whose *primary needs* are for continuing NHS health care.

The criteria set by health authorities for fully funded continuing NHS health care require evidence of a level of overall care needs (including but not limited to care from a registered nurse) leading the individual in question to have a primary need for health care and to need care beyond that which social services are able to provide under s.21 of the National Assistance Act 1948.[18] Criteria are based on the scale, range, nature, continuity and intensity of the individual's health care needs and may involve consultants, palliative care, therapy or other NHS input.

The first decision in any assessment process should always be whether or not an individual's needs meet the local criteria for fully funded continuing NHS health care and therefore whether his/her primary need is for health care. Continuing NHS health care is however only provided to residents who, because of the nature and complexity of their health care requirements, need a high level of medical and nursing care which cannot be provided outside a hospital, hospice or nursing home environment. The provision will be based upon an assessment, normally made by a consultant, on the basis of a multi-disciplinary needs assessment, prior to discharge to the care home from a hospital. Regular reassessment of the person's needs should be built into the care planning process thereafter.

Short-term nursing care[19]

There may be occasions where individuals need to go into a residential nursing home for short periods of time, for example for respite care; in an emergency or crisis (for instance if a carer or relative is suddenly taken ill and is unable to look after them); for intermediate care;[20] on a temporary placement in nursing homes under s.17 of the Mental Health Act 1983; being placed in a nursing home to await the completion of a nursing determination of care by a registered nurse; or for a trial period to explore whether they want to move into a particular care home on a permanent basis.

In these circumstances (except for intermediate care – see below) the NHS will fund nursing care under the same procedures as above, if the stay in the home is likely to last more than six weeks. For short-term placements of less than six weeks, an RNCC need not be carried out. People should be assigned to an appropriate band for the duration of their stay based on information from available records. Temporary placement in a nursing home may also be funded under funding arrangements that were in place prior to the temporary placement. For instance, if the NHS and local social services have already agreed NHS funding as part of the care package for care at home and respite care is necessary, the NHS should pay for the temporary placement under the arrangements previously agreed.

A guiding principle here should be that individuals should not be treated any less generously under these arrangements than they would otherwise have been.

Hospital admissions

When a care home resident is admitted to hospital, payments for his/her care by a registered nurse should not be duplicated for the duration of his/her stay but should resume on his/her return to the nursing home. These terms, and any variations to them, should be reflected in local NHS contracts with nursing homes. Councils and individuals will need to agree separately with nursing homes the level of fees necessary to secure the place in the nursing home in the event of such temporary absences.

Intermediate care[21]

Intermediate care covers a range of short-term treatment or rehabilitation services with appropriate care support, designed to promote independence, particularly for older people. It can be provided in a variety of settings, including a person's own home. The aim of intermediate care is to reduce the length of time that people have to stay in hospital unnecessarily when they are able to stay at or return home, and to provide services designed to ensure they are able to cope independently, both physically and emotionally, as soon as possible. Periods of intermediate care are free, and can last anything up to six weeks.[22]

WHEN WILL FREE NHS NURSING CARE BE IMPLEMENTED FOR ALL?

The new system of NHS-funded nursing care in nursing homes was introduced on 1 October 2001 for those people who were paying their own fees, known as 'self-funders'. This group includes residents who pay their fees from a variety of social security benefits, such as disability living allowance and attendance allowance. Seventy per cent of care home residents already receive care from a registered nurse paid for by the local council. These people will continue to receive free nursing funded by these resources, until the NHS takes responsibility for everyone's care from a registered nurse from April 2003. In the period between October 2001 and April 2003, all those who are assessed as needing nursing home care that need financial support from their local council will continue to have all the costs of their care (including care from qualified nurses) paid for by their local council.

CHALLENGE AND REVIEW[23]

All decisions regarding the provision of RNCC should be reviewed 3 months after their first assessment, and every 12 months thereafter, or when there is a 'significant change in their health status'. Requests for reviews outside these periods should be channelled through the nursing home co-ordinator. Individuals or their representatives, who remain dissatisfied with the care that they are receiving, should discuss this with the nursing home manager in the first instance. If this cannot be resolved, or relates to the determination of care by a registered nurse, individuals can ask the nursing home co-ordinator for a further determination to be carried out or, if still dissatisfied, for the matter to be referred to the health authority's continuing care panel (CCP) to review any determination of care by a registered nurse.

The independence or otherwise of the Continuing Care Panel, may well become a crucial issue in determining the legitimacy of any review hearing, in the light of the case of R on the Application of the Personal Representative of Christopher Beeson v Dorset CC. In this case the court decided that the rights of a person under Article 6 of the European Convention on Human Rights to a 'fair and public hearing within a reasonable time by an independent and impartial tribunal established by law, in the determination of their civil rights and obligations' had been breached when the local authority review panel consisted of two council members. Although this case concerned the review of a decision not to grant local authority support to a care home resident, on the grounds that he had too much capital, the same principle of impartiality might be applied in the context of the Continuing Care Panel.[24] (This decision was however subsequently modified by the Court of Appeal.)

COMPLAINTS

All complaints about nursing care should be addressed, in the first instance, to the internal complaints procedure that has by law to operate within each care home. This system is explained in detail in Chapter Eight at pp.118–20. Complaints may be referred to the Commission at any stage and the Commission will decide whether to investigate. It will normally only do so if the complaint has a bearing on the fitness of the service provider to continue as a registered provider. Nursing home residents should also have access to local advocacy services arranged through the NHS, councils or voluntary groups.

SERVICES AND EQUIPMENT

Care home residents should have access to the full range of specialist NHS support that is available in other care settings and to people receiving care at home, including physiotherapy, occupational therapy, speech and language therapy, dietics, podiatry and palliative care. They should not be charged for any of these services. In addition, specialist equipment needs for individual use should be addressed in the assessment and set out in the subsequent care plan, together with the arrangements for getting the equipment in place, and any after-care that may be necessary. For the majority of care home residents, much of the equipment necessary for their care will be available in the care home. Equipment may also be available on prescription from their GP, or a pre-scribing nurse, for example stoma and continence appliances, or a domiciliary oxygen therapy service. In addition to equipment that is provided or secured by the care home in accordance with the National Minimum Standards,[25] the NHS should also consider whether there is a need to provide access to hospital nutrition support teams, as well as to the full range of available community equipment services, including pressure redistributing equipment, aids to mobility, and communication aids available in other settings. Residents should have access to other NHS services, such as the wheelchair service, and staff working for the NHS should be responsible for assessing them.[26]

CONTINENCE SERVICES

Residents of care homes, including those providing nursing care, should have access to the full range of continence services provided locally.[27] As well as prevention and advice services, this should also include the provision of continence pads, which should normally only be issued after the initial assessment, or when the management plan has been completed or reviewed.[28] There is also a range of continence products available on prescription from GPs and nurse prescribers published in the Drug Tariff. All the above services should be provided free by the NHS, and without any regard to how residents' fees might be paid.

GP SERVICES

All residents of care homes should be registered with a local GP so that they can have access to the full range of NHS services that are, and must be, free for patients. Some residents wish to remain registered with their existing GP. However, the GP must be local and willing to continue providing services (i.e. within the primary care trust (PCT) covering the home or in a neighbouring PCT, where this has been formally agreed between the respective PCTs). A number of local GPs may also provide services to residents in particular homes.[29]

Although a GP may not charge NHS patients, either directly or indirectly, for the provision of general medical services, a GP may enter into arrange-ments to provide professional services to any body or institution, including nursing or residential care homes.[30] It is, for example, not unusual for a nursing or residential care home to contract for the services of a doctor for services that the NHS does not normally need to provide to patients on an individual basis, for example caring for the occupational health of the staff of the home, advising on infection control or on the management of patients with problems of mobility. It should be made clear to residents which services are provided under the GP's NHS contract, and which are additional and might need to be paid for privately. Some highly dependent patients can place greater demands on their GP. That is why the flexibilities of the National Health Service (Primary Care) Act 1997 have been used to introduce local development schemes, which are arrangements that allow health authorities or primary care groups to offer financial incentives to local GPs who provide specified services that meet local needs.[31]

ENDNOTES

1   For the distinction between law, guidance and standards see Note on Terminology. For an analysis of the linkages between inspection and registration see Cooper, J. 2002, 'Enforcing New Care Home Regulations and Standards', *Elderly Client Advisor 7* (2) 21.5.

2   Care Homes Regulations 2001, Regulation 12.

3   For definition see p.95.

4   Guidance on Free Nursing Care in Nursing Homes. HSC 2001/17: LAC (2001) 26.

5   For further information go to *www.nhfa.co.uk*

6   See Chapter Four at p.60.

7   National Health Service (Nursing Care in Residential Accommodation) (England) Directions 2001, para. 2.

8   See s.49 Health and Social Care Act 2001.

9   s.31(5).

10   Guidance on Free Nursing Care in Nursing Homes, para. 1. HSC 2001/17: LAC (2001) 26.

11   Guidance on Free Nursing Care in Nursing Homes, at p.6.

12   s.49(2) Health and Social Care Act 2001.

13   'Assessment' is defined as a process where the needs of an individual are identified and their impact on independence, daily functioning and quality of life is evaluated. This assessment should now form part of the Single Assessment Process (SAP). See Chapter Five at pp.75–76.

14   Guidance on Free Nursing Care in Nursing Homes, Appendix 6. HSC 2001/17: LAC (2001) 26.

15   Guidance on Free Nursing Care in Nursing Homes, Appendix 6. HSC 2001/17: LAC (2001) 26.

16   HSC 2001/015: LAC (2002) 18. The term replaces the previous term – 'continuing inpatient care' – which appeared to emphasise the *location* of this form of care.

17   HSC 2001/015: LAC (2002) 18.

18   See Chapter Five at p.77.

19   Guidance on Free Nursing Care in Nursing Homes, paras 5–6. HSC 2001/17: LAC (2001) 26.

20   'Intermediate care' is defined as 'a short period of active rehabilitation designed to promote recovery and the maximising of independence, normally lasting no more than six weeks'. See pp.16–23 of HSC 2001/001: LAC (2001) 1.

21   *NHS Funded Nursing Care in Nursing Homes: What it means for you.* (2001) London: DoH.

22   *NHS Funded Nursing Care in Nursing Homes: What it means for you,* citing Schedule 7 of Income Support (General) Regulations 1987, SI 1987/1967.

23   Guidance on Free Nursing Care in Nursing Homes, para. 21. HSC 2001/17: LAC (2001) 26.

24   For further details on this case see Chapter Five, p.88, and generally Chapter Seven.

25   See generally Chapter Five.

26   A Health Service circular on *Community Equipment Services* was published on 27 March 2001 and can be found at http://www.doh.gov.uk/pdfs/hsc2001008.pdf. A copy of the accompanying *Guide to Integrating Community Equipment Services* is available at http://www.doh.gov.uk/pdfs/cesguidance.pdf

27   See Standard 8 of the National Minimum Standards for Care Homes for Older People, which requires care homes to promote continence.

28   See Good Practice in Continence Services at http://www.doh.gov.uk/continenceservices.htm

29   A guide to care home managers on the services provided by GPs is available at www.doh.gov.uk/jointunit

30   The British Medical Association has published guidance for doctors on the operation of retainer fees, *Provision of Services to Registered Nursing and Residential Homes: Guidance for GPs.* (BMA, London, 1996)

31   Guidance in HSC 1999/107 included five model schemes, of which one was targeted specifically at people in nursing and residential care homes and the dependent elderly at home.

CHAPTER SEVEN

The Impact of the Human Rights Act 1998 On Care Homes

The Human Rights Act 1998 (HRA) brought the European Convention for the Protection of Human Rights and Fundamental Freedoms (the Convention) directly into UK law. As a result of the enactment of the HRA, people living in the UK can now enforce the 'Convention Rights' directly in all UK courts, rather than taking their case to the Court of Human Rights in Strasbourg. The Convention is designed to protect individuals against the power of the State, and other public authorities, by ensuring that their individual human rights are upheld.

The main objects and purposes of the Convention are:

- to be an instrument for the protection of individual human beings;

- to promote the ideals and values of a democratic society, democracy being characterised by pluralism, tolerance and broad-mindedness;

- to promote and guarantee rights that are practical and effective, rather than theoretical or illusory, and to remain a living instrument, to be interpreted in the light of present-day living conditions;

- to ensure that in its interpretation, courts reflect the increased sensitivity of the public to the fair administration of justice.

- to expect courts to give the words of the Convention their 'ordinary meaning', rather than interpret them in a way particular to a domestic jurisdiction.

Within this overall policy framework, the HRA makes it unlawful for any public authority to act in a way which is incompatible with one or more of the Convention rights (HRA s.6).

The HRA states that a public authority includes, but is not limited to, 'all courts, tribunals and any person, certain of whose functions are functions of a public nature' (HRA s.6(3)).

Public authorities will therefore include all local authority care homes. In addition, all the activities of the National Care Standards Commission (including regulation, inspection and monitoring) are those of a public authority. Whether voluntary sector homes are public authorities currently awaits the outcome of an important test case, involving care homes run by the Leonard Cheshire Foundation. In June 2001, the High Court in London ruled that the Foundation was not a public authority for the purposes of the Human Rights Act as it did not exercise a 'public function' in relation to care home residents. The decision was upheld on appeal in 2002. The outcome of this case impacts upon the question: Are the activities of a private care home subject to the Human Rights Act? In essence, it seems increasingly likely that the rights of residents in all care homes will sooner or later come under the protection of the Human Rights Act as the increased intervention of public funding and public regulation moves care homes ever closer to the overarching concept of a 'public authority'.

WHO CAN TAKE ACTION UNDER THE HRA?

Any person, organisation or group of individuals claiming to be directly affected by a public authority's breach of a Convention right (or rights) (described as a 'victim') can take legal action against the public authority responsible for the act (or omission) leading to the breach. Thus any resident or employee of a care home that meets the test of a public authority is a potential victim. A deceased person's relatives may bring proceedings on behalf of a victim where a complaint is made about that person's death, or if the victim is alive, but lacks legal capacity to litigate (a child, for example) a relative can also bring proceedings on his/her behalf.

WHAT ARE THE HUMAN RIGHTS THAT THE CONVENTION SEEKS TO PROTECT?

The human rights that the Convention protects are broadly divided into three categories: *absolute rights*, *limited rights*, and *qualified rights*. The full text of most of the cases cited below can be read and downloaded from the European Court of Human Rights website.[1] (Where an endnote reference is provided this is normally because the full text of the case is not available on the website.)

Absolute rights

These are rights that cannot be restricted in any circumstances. Those which may be relevant in the care home sector are:

Article 2: The right to life and the prohibition of arbitrary deprivation of life.

Comment: It is likely that the decision-making processes operating in the NHS with regard to giving or refusing treatment will come under much greater scrutiny, particularly when a failure to provide treatment may lead to a person's death, thereby triggering the protection of Article 2. Health authorities and trusts should identify these potential areas early if it is necessary to take action now, for example because important policy or operational considerations are at stake. In circumstances where a public authority such as the NHS fails to provide people with life-saving treatment, or fails to provide them with the care necessary to stop them taking their own lives, it is arguable that the public authority in question will have breached Article 2. Note however that although the State has a positive obligation to protect the lives of its citizens *if this is in the patient's best interests* (*Osman v UK* (1999)[2]), this positive obligation is not absolute. It only requires the State to take 'adequate and appropriate measures' to protect life (see *Association X v UK*,[3] which concerned a vaccination programme).

It has been argued that where a council closes down one of its own care homes in such a way that could hasten the death of any of the residents, Article 2 protection may be invoked. Several cases of this natute have commenced, although in most cases they have reached out of court settlements, or have been adjourned to enable local authorities to take alternative courses of action. In many instances an alternative action under Article 8 may be preferable.[4]

Article 3: The prohibition of torture, inhuman or degrading treatment or punishment.

'Degrading treatment' refers to behaviour which arouses in the victim a feeling of fear, anguish and inferiority, capable of humiliating and debasing the victim and possibly breaking his or her physical or moral resistance. 'Inhuman treatment' is treatment that causes intense physical pain or entails suffering. 'Torture' is deliberate inhuman treatment that causes very serious and cruel suffering.

Comment: A number of existing health and community care practices must run the risk of an imminent challenge under Article 3. It has been established, for example, that lack of proper medical care in a case where someone is suffering from a serious illness could in certain circumstances amount to inhuman or degrading treatment, contrary to Article 3 (*Tanko v Finland* (1994)). If a person in the advanced stages of an incurable disease is threatened with deportation to a country unable to treat or care for victims of this disease, his/her Article 3 rights may be breached (*D v UK* (1997)). Treatment will be inhuman if it causes 'intense physical or mental suffering' (*Ireland v UK* (1976)) or 'feelings of fear, anguish and inferiority capable of humiliating and debasing them and possibly breaking their physical or moral resistance' (*Ireland v UK* (1976)). Conversely, measures taken out of therapeutic necessity cannot be regarded as inhuman or degrading treatment, so long as the medical necessity for the measures has been convincingly shown to exist (*Herczegafalvy v Austria* (1993)[5]). Where a person has been deprived of their liberty, the threshold for inhuman treatment is lowered (*Tomasi v France* (1992)[6]), and the vulnerability of the person is also a relevant factor: *Ribitsch v Austria* (1992)[7].

Comment: It is arguable that many people in care homes have effectively lost their liberty, thus bringing them into the special categories of vulnerability outlined in the above cases, thereby increasing the levels of responsibility of their care homes to protect their human rights. In one English local authority, a new environmentally friendly policy of providing reusable incontinence pads to adults with learning difficulties was introduced, with the consequence that users of the pads were obliged on occasion to sit in their own urine or faeces for several hours a day. When faced with a legal challenge under Article 3, the authority backed down, and settled the case prior to the issue of proceedings. The practice still however continues elsewhere. In another case, the defendant authority was threatening to close a special care home for children with severe autism, who experience episodes of extremely violent and anti-social behaviour. There was strong evidence before the court that if the home were to be closed, the children would suffer lasting psychological damage, and would also have to be placed in full-time council care. In the face of a strong Article 3 argument, the case was adjourned to permit the council to give further consideration to the funding issue, and the council backed down from the closure.[8]

Limited rights

These are rights containing a clause that sets out particular circumstances in which the right may be infringed without breaching the Article. It is unlikely that any issue concerning these rights will arise in a care home, as they are concerned generally with the trial process, forms of lawful detention, and with the right to marry.

There is however one area where a care home may be vulnerable to challenge under the limited rights provisions. This is where a resident feels that s/he has been deprived of a civil right or obligation without access to any independent and impartial tribunal where s/he can challenge the decision. In a recent case, Dorset County Council determined that a care home resident had deliberately deprived himself of capital in order to avoid making a contribution to the cost of his care home accommodation. The High Court decided that their internal appeals procedure failed to provide the resident, or his relative, with an independent and impartial tribunal in which to challenge the decision, and thereby breached his rights under Article 6.[9] Whether a similar challenge might be mounted against the level of nursing care provision being provided to the resident remains ro be seen.[10]

Qualified rights

These are rights which, although set out in positive form, can be lawfully restricted, but only if:

1.   There is a domestic law in force permitting the restriction that is clear and sufficiently precise to enable a citizen to regulate his or her conduct accordingly.

2.   The restriction is 'necessary in a democratic society', and 'proportionate'.

> The term 'necessary' does not have the flexibility of such expressions as 'useful' or 'desirable'. In addition, pluralism, tolerance and broadmindedness are hallmarks of a 'democratic society'. Although individual interests must on occasion be subordinated to those of a group, democracy does not simply mean that the views of a majority must always prevail: a balance must be achieved which ensures the fair and proper treatment of minorities and avoids any abuse of a dominant position. (*Chassagnou v France* (1999) p.112)

> Every formality, condition, restriction, or penalty imposed in this sphere must be proportionate to the legitimate aim pursued. (*Handyside v UK* (1976) p.49)[11]

3.   The restriction is not 'discriminatory' (see Article 14 below).

4.   The restriction falls within one, or more, of the 'permitted aims' set out in the Convention.

Permitted Aims

1. It reflects the interests of national security.

2. It protects public safety or the economic well-being of the country.

3. It prevents disorder or crime.

4. It protects health, morals, or the rights and freedoms of others.

The qualified rights which are most likely to be invoked in care home settings are:

> Article 8: The right to respect for private and family life, home and correspondence

Comment: Under Article 8, all people have the right to respect for their private and family life, their home and their correspondence. The notion of 'private life' is 'a broad one and not susceptible to exhaustive definition' (*Niemitz v Germany* (1992), *Costello-Roberts v UK* (1993)). It extends to the development of relationships with others, including business and professional relations. 'It is after all in the course of their working lives that the majority of people have a significant, if not the greatest, opportunity of developing relationships with others' (*Niemitz v Germany* (1992)).

Article 8 imposes positive obligations to take action to secure the right, although such action must balance the rights of the individual against the interest of the community at large (*Rees v UK* (1986)). One consequence of this provision is that budgetary restraints might not be sufficient reason for inactivity where a right is being breached.

Personal sexuality and sexual activity are both protected by Article 8 (*Dudgeon v UK* (1981)).

There have already been several Article 8 cases decided in the forum of the ECHR at Strasbourg, that illustrate how the HRA might be applied to the provision of community care services in the UK. In the case of *Botta v Italy* (1998), Mr Botta and his friend, who were both physically disabled, went on holiday to the seaside resort of Lido degli Estenzo, in the province of Ferrara. On arrival, they discovered that the beaches were privately run on licence from the local authority (a common practice in Italian resorts) and were not equipped with the facilities needed to enable disabled people to gain access to the beach and the sea (i.e. such aids as access ramps and disabled toilets and washrooms). Mr Botta subsequently filed a complaint at the ECHR arguing that the failure of the Ferrara local authorities (and public prosecutor's office) to enforce the requirement on the licensee to ensure that such facilities were available to disabled people amounted to a breach of Article 8 (and of Article 14). Although Mr Botta lost his case before the ECHR, (for reasons see paragraph 4 below), the Court made a number of important observations in connection with the scope of Article 8, as follows:

1.   Private life includes a person's physical and psychological integrity. The guarantee afforded by Article 8 is primarily intended to ensure the development, without outside interference, of the personality of each individual in his/her relations with other human beings.

2.   While the essential object of Article 8 is to protect the individual against arbitrary interference by a public authority, it does not merely compel the State to abstain from such interference. In addition to this negative undertaking, there may be positive obligations inherent in effective respect for private or family life. These obligations may involve the adoption of measures designed to secure respect for private life even in the sphere of the relations of individuals between themselves.

3.   Positive obligations of the type described above are however limited to situations where there is clearly a direct and immediate link between the measures sought by applicants, and their private and/or family lives.

4.   In the case of Mr Botta, the Court decided that the right to gain access to a beach, during his holidays, at a place distant from his normal place of residence, concerned 'interpersonal relations of such broad and indeterminate scope' that there could be no conceivable direct link between his private life and the measures he argues the local authority ought to have taken.

Article 8 was argued in another recent case, also against the Government of Italy: *Marzari v Italy* (1999). In this case the applicant suffered from a series of complex disabilities. He filed an action against the government for failing to provide him with accommodation suitable for a person with his disabilities. The applicant was unsuccessful because the court decided that the state had taken all reasonable steps to provide him with suitable accommodation, which he had rejected, notwithstanding the fact that an independent tribunal had determined that the accommodation was suitable, with modification. Although the applicant lost his case on the facts, the court nevertheless left the door open for a different outcome, had the facts been more compellingly in favour of the applicant, stating that 'although Article 8 does not guarantee to have one's [housing] problems solved by the authorities, a refusal of the authorities to provide assistance in this respect to an individual suffering from a severe disease might in certain circumstances raise an issue under Article 8, because of the impact of such refusal on the private life of the individual'.

There are a number of situations in which an Article 8 challenge has succeeded:

1.   *Airey v Ireland* (1979): The applicant successfully argued that the failure of the state to provide her with an affordable legal representative in a complex legal separation case to which she was a party, but the complexity of which she could not understand, directly affected her private and family life.

2.   *X and Y v The Netherlands* (1985): A mentally handicapped woman who had been raped, successfully argued that the Netherlands Criminal Code had not provided her with practical and effective protection (her uncorroborated evidence was inadmissible), and had thereby directly affected her private and family life.

3.   *Lopez Ostra v Spain* (1994): This case concerned the harmful effects of pollution caused by the activity of a waste-water treatment plant situated near the applicant's home. It was held that the State had not succeeded in striking a fair balance between the interest of the town of Lorca's economic well-being, and the applicant's enjoyment of her right to respect for her home and her private and family life.

4.   *Guerra v Italy* (1998): In this case it was held that the danger of the direct effects of toxic emissions from a nearby factory had not been adequately communicated to the applicant family, thereby directly failing to respect their right to private and family life.

5.   *Halford v UK* (1997): A senior police officer, under investigation for disciplinary offences, discovered that private communications from her office to her home were being monitored. It was held that interception of communications constitutes an interference with the right to private life and correspondence, both at home and at work, unless justified by law. In contrast, the applicant in *Acmanne v Belgium* (1993) failed to establish that compulsory TB screening was a breach of Article 8. Such testing was held to be a justified interference in his private life, to protect health.

6.   Whenever a seriously disabled person in residential care is moved
       to different accommodation it is likely that Article 8 questions
       will arise (*R v North and East Devon Health Authority, ex p. Coughlan*
       (1999)[12]). This is regardless of the reason for the move. The local
       authority must show that it has balanced all relevant issues one
       against the other (risk to the resident in staying, threat to his/her
       family life in moving, costs of both and so forth) and decided that
       there is an overriding reason which permits it to place a restriction
       on, and thereby infringe, the individual's Article 8 rights. It is
       worth noting that if the move could lead to the premature death
       of, for example, a frail older person, there could also be an
       infringement of Article 2. Challenges to a move have tended to be
       grounded in contractual promises, of a 'home for life', which have
       led the court to conclude that the resident had a 'legitimate
       expectation to remain there for the rest of their life': (*R v Camden
       LBC ex p. Bodimeade and others* (2001).[13]

7.   Medical records fall within the sphere of private life, and therefore
       any restriction on patients' access to their records is only
       permissible if justified as both necessary and proportionate (*Gaskin
       v UK* (1989)), as the right to information about your development
       is a component of Article 8. In a care home this issue may arise
       when residents lack the mental capacity to ask to see the medical
       (or any written) records referring to them, which would otherwise
       be their entitlement under the Data Protection Act.

8.   As medical confidentiality is considered to be crucial both to the
       privacy of the individual and to preserving confidence in the
       medical and health professions, any disclosure in breach of this
       confidentiality must be rarely permissible, and then only in very
       tightly controlled circumstances, to avoid a breach of Article 8 (*Z
       v Finland* (1997)).

9.   Making unsubstantiated allegations about a person's private life
       (in this case allegations of sex abuse disclosed by the police to an
       employer) is likely to be a breach of Article 8 (*R v Local Authority
       and Police Authority in the Midlands, ex p. L.M.* (2000)).[14]

10.   Note that a stable relationship between same-sex couples is
       protected under Article 8 as 'private life' (*X and Y v UK* (1983)).[15]

> Article 9: Freedom of thought, conscience and religion, including the right to manifest religion or belief in public or private worship, teaching, practice and observation.

Comment: Under Article 9 everyone has the right to freedom of thought, conscience and religion, either alone or in community with others, and in public or private, to manifest their religion or belief or worship, teaching, practice and observation. Article 9 protects the sphere of personal beliefs and religious creeds. In addition it protects acts that are intimately linked to these attitudes, such as acts of worship or devotion which are aspects of the practice of a religion or belief in a generally recognised form (*C v UK* (1983)).[16] There are a number of specific circumstances in which the ability to practice one's faith is of fundamental importance to a person. For example, the right under Article 9 to a kosher diet for prisoners has been upheld: (*D.S. and E.S. v UK* (1990)).[17] A public authority may therefore need to take positive steps to ensure a right is not violated. Such measures may, in certain circumstances, constitute a legal means of ensuring that an individual will not be disturbed in their worship by the acts of others (*Dubowska and Skup v Poland* (1997)).[18] It is arguable that a failure to provide individuals in a care home with transport provision to attend a place of worship, when they are otherwise immobile, or failing to provide them with food that forms part of their religious practices, or with facilities in their home to observe their religious needs, could amount to a breach of Article 9.

Finally, note that 'religion' is construed very widely under the Convention, and has been held to include in addition to mainstream religions, Druidism, the Divine Light Zentrum, the Krishna Consciousness Movement and the Church of Scientology.

> Article 10: Freedom of expression, including the right to receive and impart information and ideas without interference

> Article 14: The enjoyment of the rights and freedoms set forth in this Convention shall be secured without discrimination on any ground such as sex, race, colour, language, religion, political or other opinion, national or social origin, association with a national minority, property, birth, or other status.

Comment: It should be noted however that Article 14 is not free-standing, in that it only applies to the rights and freedoms already contained in the Convention. This means that in practice Article 14 can only be invoked in conjunction with another of the Convention Rights, and cannot therefore be invoked in isolation. A breach of Article 14 can however be established, even if the breach of the accompanying right is not established: (*Abdulaziz, Cabales and Balkandali v UK* (1985)).

Under Article 14 discrimination means 'a difference in treatment which has no reasonable or objective justification'. Any such justification will depend upon whether a legitimate aim for the measure can be made out, and whether the discriminatory means employed are proportionate to the aim. The categories of discrimination are not closed, i.e. other status is deliberately open to new categories such as disability (*Malone v UK* (1996)). Article 14 is also violated when a state fails to treat differently persons whose situations are significantly different, e.g. prisoners of conscience as compared to ordinary criminals (*Thlimmennos v Greece* (2000)).

ENDNOTES

1　www.echr.coe.int
2　*The Times*, 5 November 1999. See also *Edwards v UK*, 2001.
3　No. 7154/75, 14 DR 31.
4　For information and advice on these and other cases being brought under the Human Rights Act in this field contact Nicola Mackintosh, Mackintosh Duncan, 103 Borough High St, London SE1 1NL. Tel: 0207 357 6464.
5　15 EHRR 437.
6　'Although the injuries observed might appear to be relatively slight, they nevertheless constituted outward signs of the use of physical force on an individual deprived of his (or her) liberty and therefore in a state of inferiority. The treatment has therefore been both inhuman and degrading.'
7　'In respect of a person deprived of his (or her) liberty, any recourse to physical force which has not been made strictly necessary by his or her own conduct diminishes human dignity and is, in principle, an infringement of...Article 3.
8　See Note 4 above.
9　*R on the Application of the Personal Representatives of Christopher Beeson v Dorset County Council*, Case No: C0/25/2001.
10　See Chapter Five at p.93.
11　1 EHRR 1.
12　2 CCLR 285. See also Note 4 above.
13　4 CCLR 246.
14　1 FLR 612.
15　32 DR 220.
16　37 DR 147.

17   65 DR 245.
18   24 EHRR CD 75.

CHAPTER EIGHT

Complaints Procedures, Rights of Appeal and the Care Homes Tribunal

This chapter will examine the range of complaints and appeals procedures that are available in the care homes world, both to residents and to registered owners and managers.

Complaints are most effective if they can provide evidence that a requirement or expectation has not been met, in circumstances where it would be reasonable to meet them. To assist in this process of clarification, the registered provider or registered manager of the home has a legal duty to produce a written guide to the care home – *a service user's guide* – containing the following information:[1]

- A summary of the *statement of purpose* of the home.
- The terms and conditions in respect of accommodation to be provided for residents, including the amount and method of payment of fees.
- A standard form of contract for the provision of services and facilities by the home to the resident.
- The most recent inspection report.
- A summary of the complaints procedures established under Regulation 22.
- The address and telephone number of the Commission: St Nicholas Building, St. Nicholas St, Newcastle NE1 1NB.

The statement of purpose is a written statement of the aims and objectives of the care home, the facilities and services which are to be provided to the residents, and specific details on each of the following: the name and address of the registered provider and of any registered manager; the relevant qualifications and experience of the registered provider and any registered manager; the number, relevant qualifications and experience of the staff working at the care home; the organisational structure of the care home; the age-range and sex of the residents for whom it is intended that accommodation should be provided; the range of needs that the care home is intended to meet; whether nursing is to be provided; any criteria used for admission to the care home, including the care home's policy and procedures (if any) for emergency admissions; the arrangements for residents to engage in social activities, hobbies and leisure interests; the arrangements made for consultation with residents about the operation of the care home; the fire precautions and associated emergency procedures in the care home; the arrangements made for residents to attend religious services of their choice; the arrangements made for contact between residents and their relatives, friends and representatives; the arrangements for dealing with reviews of the service user's plan;[2] the number and size of rooms in the care home; details of any specific therapeutic techniques used in the care home and arrangements for their supervision; the arrangements for respecting the privacy and dignity of residents.

A copy of the service user's guide must be lodged with the National Care Standards Commission. Both the service user's guide and the statement of purpose must be kept under review, and revised where appropriate. The Commission must be informed of any such revisions. The statement of purpose must also include a statement of the arrangements for dealing with complaints.[3]

COMPLAINTS PROCEDURES FOR CARE HOME RESIDENTS, THEIR REPRESENTATIVES, FRIENDS AND RELATIVES

Internal complaints procedure

In general terms, complaints procedures should be designed to provide an effective means of allowing residents or their representatives to complain about the quality or nature of the service and to ensure complaints are acted upon. Care homes should always aim to resolve complaints quickly and as close to the point of service delivery as is acceptable and appropriate, and to give those denied a service an accepted means of challenging the decision made.

Care Homes Regulation 22 sets out the legal requirements placed upon care homes regarding complaints procedures for residents. Under this Regulation the registered person must establish a complaints procedure, for considering complaints made to the registered person by a resident, or person acting on the resident's behalf, as follows:

1.   The complaints procedure must be appropriate to the needs of the care home residents.

2.   The registered person must supply a written copy of the complaints procedure to every resident, and to any person acting on behalf of a service user if that person so requests. The written copy of the complaints procedure must include the name and address and telephone numebr of the National Care Standards Commission, and the procedure (if any) that has been notified by the Commission to the registered person for the making of complaints to the Commission relating to the care home. Where the recipient of the written complaints procedure is blind or visually impaired the registered person should supply in addition, and so far as it is practicable to do so, a version of the procedure in suitable format.

3.   On receiving a complaint from a resident, or in connection with a resident, the registered person must within 28 days or such shorter period as may be reasonable in the circumstances, inform the person who made the complaint of the action (if any) that is to be taken, and must ensure that any complaint made under this procedure is fully investigated.

4.   The registered person must supply to the Commission, if so requested, a statement containing a summary of the complaints made during the preceding 12 months and the action that was taken.

In addition, the National Minimum Standards set out the following provisions regarding the handling of complaints in care homes:

Standard 16

Outcome: Residents and their relatives and friends are confident that their complaints will be listened to, taken seriously and acted upon.

Process: The care home must have a simple, clear and accessible complaints procedure that is capable of responding to all complaints within 28 days. A record must be kept of all complaints made, including details of investigations and any action taken.

Standard 17

Outcome: Residents' legal rights are protected.

Process: Specifically, where service users lack capacity, the care home must facilitate access to advocacy services.[4] Also, steps must be taken to ensure that residents are able to vote in elections. This list is not, however, exhaustive.

Standard 18

Outcome: Residents are protected from abuse.

Process: The full text of this requirement reads as follows: 'service users [must be] safeguarded from physical, financial or material, psychological or sexual abuse, neglect, discriminatory abuse or self-harm, inhuman or degrading treatment, through deliberate intent, negligence or ignorance, in accordance with written policies'. The impact of the Human Rights Act will also play a key role in maintaining this standard (see generally Chapter Seven). The home must demonstrate that it has in place 'robust procedures' for responding to any suspicions concerning possible abuse, including safeguards against staff seeking to gain some financial gain from involvement with a resident.

Complaint to the local authority social services department, the NHS or the health authority

If residents, or their representatives ('complainants'), are unhappy with any aspect of the service that they have received from the social services department they should complain to the relevant social services department, which must have, by law, a formal complaints procedure in place. If the complainant remains dissatisfied after the social services complaints procedure has been completed, s/he should contact the local authority commissioner (ombudsman).[5]

If the residents/representatives wish to make a complaint about service or treatment received from the National Health Service, they should, wherever possible, talk in the first instance to someone close to the cause of the complaint – the doctor, nurse, receptionist or practice manager, for example.[6] The Patient's Charter sets out the principal patients' rights, together with the standards of service they can expect to receive from the National Health Service in England (Scotland, Wales and Northern Ireland have their own separate Charters). It also sets out how patients can complain if they are not satisfied with the service provided.[7]

If complainants remain dissatisfied, they can ask for a review of their complaint by an independent panel. If their request is granted, the review will be carried out by a panel, usually composed of three members. The panel will be chaired by an independent person. Each health authority will have a leaflet explaining these procedures, a copy of which should be available in every care home.

Patient advocacy liaison service (PALS)

Since April 2002, trusts running hospitals, GP practices and frontline community health services must operate a patient advocacy and liaison service (PALS). Patients and carers are encouraged to use PALS whenever they have a problem to resolve or wish to air concerns about the treatment, care or support they are receiving. PALS have direct access to the trust's chief executive, and the power to negotiate an immediate solution, in addition to more formal procedures for mediating complaints and disputes.

Ombudsman services

There are two ombudsman services that may be relevant to residents in care homes who wish to make a complaint about a service they have or have not received. The first ombudsman is described as the local authority commissioner (the LAC).[8] LACs have the power to investigate individual complaints against local authorities, alleging maladministration, which includes undue delay, bias, discrimination, failure to apply rules of procedure, and general misconduct or incompetence. This would therefore cover complaints concerning such matters as maladminstration in the processing of an application for residential care, including both the primary assessment and the stages thereafter. Ombudsman investigations are, however, notoriously slow and time-consuming. They are also thoroughly probing, giving ombudsmen extensive powers to demand access to internal documentation, and interview any individuals concerned with a particular case. The investigation, which can typically take up to one year, concludes in a written report, setting out the ombudsman's findings, which is publicly available. If there is a finding against the local authority of maladministration, the report may suggest an appropriate form of compensation, although this is not legally enforceable.

The parallel ombudsman who has the power to investigate failings to individual patients in the health service is the health services ombudsman (the HSO).[9] The HSO will not become involved unless complainants have taken up their complaints officially, under the complaints procedures described above, but remain dissatisfied, for example because it took too long to deal with the complaint locally, because they were unreasonably refused a panel review, or because they did not get a satisfactory answer to their complaint.[10]

Judicial review of a decision

Judicial review is a procedure whereby the High Court reviews the legality of the decision of a public body or public authority. This procedure is only available in challenges against a decision of such bodies. Chapter Seven reviews the meaning of the term 'public body/public authority'.[11] It is currently the case that whilst local authorities and the National Care Standards Commission are clearly in this category, privately run care homes are probably not. Judicial review of a decision is triggered by an application seeking leave in the Divisional Court to apply for judicial review, which can be funded by legal aid, subject to a means test. The application must be lodged within three months of the date when it is alleged that the grounds of appeal arose. If leave is granted, on the basis that there is evidence of a case to answer, a full judicial review hearing will be ordered, though it will normally be many months before the actual hearing. Judicial review cases are expensive, costing respondent bodies many thousands of pounds even if they have a successful outcome, and are to be avoided if at all possible. Having looked at the evidence, it is open for the court to find against the local authority on all or any of the following grounds:

Illegality. This means that the public body in question had no power to make the decision that it made, or that it was wrong in law. Thus a failure to carry out a statutory duty, or to follow statutory guidance (LASSA), may lead to a finding of illegality. Similarly unlawful fettering of discretion, unlawful delegation of powers or duties to a third party, and unlawfully narrowing the care criteria based upon a misunderstanding of what local authorities are able to purchase, may all be declared illegal.

Procedural impropriety. This means that the public body's decision was unfair, because either the complainant was denied a consultation to which s/he was entitled, or the decision was taken in breach of the 'rules of natural justice', which require that both sides of an argument should be heard before a decision is reached, and that the decision should be free from any bias. A failure to give reasons for reaching a decision may well be seen as a procedural impropriety, as may be a failure to follow laid down procedures.

Irrationality. This means that a public body has taken a decision, or failed to act, in a way that no rational public body could have done, or in other words, it has 'taken leave of its senses', a line of conduct 'which no sensible authority acting with due appreciation for its responsibilities would have decided to adopt'.[12]

Finally, it should be noted that if the applicant wins his/her case against the public body in question, and the court makes a finding of illegality, procedural impropriety or irrationality, the matter does not rest there. The court will normally simply quash the original decision and refer the case back to the local authority for reconsideration. So long as the new decision does not offend any of the above principles, that will be the end of the matter.

Obtaining evidence in support of a complaint: obtaining access to written records

If a resident, or a close friend or relative of a resident, wishes to raise an issue about the care of the resident that may lead to a formal complaint, it will often be important for him/her to have access to written records about the resident's care that are in the possession of the care home management, the social services department or the health authority.

It may be that the home or authority willingly provides details of the written records associated with the resident's care on request. But if this is not the case, the Data Protection Act 1998 provides individuals (described as 'data subjects') with extensive rights of access to any records referring to them, on request. The right of access applies both to records stored on a computer, and to manual records.

To obtain a copy of a written record concerning him/herself, the resident, or person acting on his/her behalf, has to make a written request to the person nominated by the home or the authority as their 'data controller'.[13] Requests must be addressed 'promptly', and in any event within 40 days of receipt of the request.[14] In certain circumstances a fee (maximum £10) can be charged for providing the information.

There are a number of limited circumstances in which the data controller may refuse access to the data subject, of which the following examples may be relevant in a care home:

1. Information covered by legal professional privilege (e.g. correspondence between the home and the home's solicitor).

2. Information as to the physical or mental health or condition of the data subject, to the extent that its release would be likely to cause serious harm to the physical or mental health or condition of the data subject or any other person. This right of refusal is however limited and subject to safeguards. First, if the data

controller is not a health professional, s/he must have or seek a recent opinion from a health professional in support of the refusal. Second, s/he can only withhold that part of the record believed to be seriously harmful, and must reveal the rest of the record. Third, the threshold is high, i.e. mere harm or distress is insufficient. It must be an objective risk that it will be serious.

3.   Where release would lead to the disclosure of information relating to a third party who can be identified from that information. This exemption does *not* apply if the third party is a health professional or a person carrying out social service functions in connection with the case.

There is a potential problem concerning obtaining records on behalf of a person who has lost the mental capacity to give consent to the request, as, under the Data Protection Act, the only person entitled to receive the information is the data subject, or a person acting on his/her behalf, *with his/her consent*, e.g. a solicitor. In these circumstances, it *may* be possible to argue that denying an incapacitated resident the right of access to records in these circumstances breaches his/her human rights under the Human Rights Act. This argument can only be used, however, if the home in question is a 'public authority' within the meaning of the Act.[15]

RIGHTS OF CARE HOME OWNERS TO APPEAL AGAINST ADVERSE DECISIONS

Review by the National Care Standards Commission

We have already noted in Chapter Three that the National Care Standards Commission, and in certain circumstances the Magistrates' Court, can impose conditions upon the operation of care homes, and ultimately close them down. This section examines the various appeals procedures that are available to the registered owners of care homes in these circumstances.

The Commission can give any person registered in respect of a residential care home notice of a proposal to cancel the registration under a number of grounds or a notice concerning a proposal to vary or impose conditions upon registration. Where such a notice is served, the scheme of the Act provides for the recipient of that notice to have the opportunity to make representations to the Commission concerning the matter.[16] Appeal against any adverse decision of an inspector lies, in the first instance, to the Commission direct. The appeal must be made by way of written representations within 28 days of notice of the adverse decision being communicated to the owner or manager of the home. The appeal will be handled by the Commission at the regional level, though this will probably be in a different region from the one in which the home is located. The Care Standards Act sets no time limit for the adjudication of this appeal, but normal principles of public law and natural justice would suggest that this must be within a reasonable time.

If, following this process, the decision of the inspector is upheld, a further appeal against that decision (or alternatively against an order made by a JP[17]) lies to the Care Standards Tribunal. No appeal against a decision or order may be brought, however, more than 28 days after service on the care home manager of notice of the decision of the Commission, or the JP in the Magistrates' Court.

On an appeal against a decision of the Commission, the Tribunal may confirm the decision or direct that it shall not have effect. On an appeal against an order made by a JP, the tribunal may confirm the order or direct that it shall cease to have effect. The procedure has not, in the past, been speedy. Under the previous regime, the average time from first decision to Tribunal hearing was about 12 months.

Appeal to the Care Standards Tribunal

Since April 2002, The Care Standards Tribunal[18] has replaced the Registered Homes Tribunal as the tribunal dealing with all the above matters. Appeals to the Tribunal arise under the Care Standards Act.[19] Each appeal is heard separately by a specifically convened Tribunal. The Tribunal will be the same body as provided for in the Protection of Children Act 1999, but for the purposes of its functions to hear appeals under the Care Standards Act it will be referred to as the Care Standards Tribunal (CST). A Tribunal can hear more than one appeal at the same time in certain circumstances, providing the appellant and the Chair of the Tribunal agree to this. The circumstances are:

1.   where the appeals relate to the same care home; *or*

2.   where appeals relate to different homes, but the appellant is the same.

The Tribunal operates under the Care Standards Act 2000 and the Tribunal Regulations 2002.[20] All its decisions are published, and can be read and downloaded on the DoH website.[21] The Tribunal Chair is appointed by the Lord Chancellor, and has legal qualifications. The other two members of the Tribunal are lay experts, and will have qualifications or expertise relevant to the type of home that is the subject of the appeal. Tribunals normally sit in a location near the home that is the subject of the appeal, although they can take place in other locations. The overall responsibility for allocating members to Tribunals rests with the Tribunal President.

The CST will hear appeals in England and Wales against decisions of the National Care Standards Commission (England) and the National Assembly (Wales) in respect of care homes. The Tribunal Regulations 2002 provide a core set of procedural rules that provide for the overall management of appeal cases and the direction-making powers of the Tribunal President and of the Tribunal. These include provisions for:

- the constitution of the Tribunal;[22]
- the appointment of Tribunal members to hear particular appeal cases;[23]
- the fixing of a date for the hearing and other arrangements for the hearing;[24]
- enabling appeals to be heard together where two or more appeals concern the same person;[25]
- the determination of appeals without an oral hearing, where requested by the appellant;[26]
- preliminary hearings, where appropriate;[27]
- issuing of costs warnings and costs orders, where there is no hope of succeeding and the party has acted unreasonably in bringing or conducting the appeal;[28]
- enabling the Chair to direct the date by which relevant information and evidence must be submitted or exchanged between the parties;[29]
- determining how evidence will be taken and presented in relation to vulnerable adults;[30]
- the actual procedure during the hearing. The Regulations state that 'the Tribunal may regulate its own procedure';[31]
- the Tribunal's decision-making process;[32]
- the power of the President to strike out any appeal that is misconceived;[33]
- the power to make restricted reporting orders.[34]

Review of the Tribunal's decision

After the outcome of the hearing, either party can apply to the Secretary to the Tribunal requesting that the Tribunal's decision be reviewed, on any of the following grounds:

(a) It was wrongly made, as a result of an error on the part of the Tribunal staff.

(b) A party, who was entitled to be heard at a hearing but failed to appear or to be represented, had good and sufficient reason for failing to appear.

(c) There was an obvious error in the decision.

(d) The interests of justice so require.

An application to review a decision must be made not later than 10 working days after the date on which the decision was sent to the party applying for the decision to be reviewed, and must be in writing, stating the grounds in full. The application may be refused by the President, or by the Chair of the Tribunal which decided the case, if in his/her opinion it has no reasonable prospect of success. If it is not refused on these grounds, the application will be heard and determined once again, by the Tribunal which decided the case or, where that is not practicable, by another Tribunal appointed by the President.[35]

Having reviewed all or part of a decision the Tribunal may set aside or vary the decision by a certificate signed by the Chair[36] and substitute such other decision as it thinks fit, or order a rehearing before the same or a differently constituted Tribunal.

If any decision is set aside or varied (whether as a result of a review or by order of the High Court) the Secretary shall alter the relevant entry in the records to conform to the Chair's certificate or the order of the High Court and shall notify the parties accordingly.

ENDNOTES

1   The Care Homes Regulations 2001, Regulation 5.

2   See Chapter Four at pp.59–60.

3   The Care Homes Regulations 2001, Schedule 1.

4   This will normally be done through the PALS, see p.121.

5   See p.121.

6   A leaflet, *Complaints: Listening..Acting..Improving*, is available in a variety of languages, free of charge, from the Health Literature Line (Freephone 0800-555777). It explains in more detail how the NHS complaints procedure works.

7   Copies of the Charter may be obtained by writing to Department of Health, PO Box 777, London SE1 6XH. Fax: 01623 724 524.

8   The LGOs derive their authority from the Local Government Act 1974, as amended by Local Government and Housing Act 1989.

9   For detailed information about the HSO, including a summary of the most important recent decisions, visit www.ombudsman.org.uk/hse

10 For a substantial digest of the most important recent decisions of local government ombudsmen relevant to this area consult Mandelstam, M. (1999) *Community Care Practice and the Law.* Second edition. London: Jessica Kingsley Publishers, Chapter 18, 459–542; or *The Annual Digests of Cases,* available from Local Government Ombudsman, 21 Queen Anne's Gate, London SW1H 9AT.

11 See Chapter Seven at pp.105–6.

12 *R v Secretary of State for Education and Science v Tameside Metropolitan Borough Council* (1977) AC 1014. See also *R on the Application of Daly and Home Secretary* (2001) 3 All ER 433.

13 Every institution holding data on another has to nominate their data controller.

14 s.7(8)(10) Data Protection Act.

15 See Chapter Seven at pp.105–6 for more detail on this point.

16 s.17–18 CSA. This does not however confer a right to a full hearing before the Commission, or the right to cross-examine local authority officers (*R v Leicestershire CC ex p. Thompson* (2000) 3 CCLR 45).

17 See Chapter Two at p.27 for details of this procedure.

18 This is not the full legal title of the Tribunal, which is POCAT, but it has been adopted as the working title for the time being.

19 s.21 CSA.

20 The Protection of Children and Vulnerable Adults and Care Standards Tribunal Regulations 2002.

21 www.doh.gov.uk/rht/guide1.htm

22 Tribunal Regulation 5.

23 Tribunal Regulation 5.

24 Tribunal Regulation 7.

25 Tribunal Regulation 8.

26 Tribunal Regulation 6.

27 Tribunal Regulation 6.

28 Tribunal Regulation 10.

29 Tribunal Regulation 6.

30 Tribunal Regulation 18.

31 Tribunal Regulation 21.

32 Tribunal Regulation 24.

33 Tribunal Regulations, Schedule 1 para. 4.

34 Tribunal Regulation 19.

35 Note that the Tribunal may, on its own initiative, propose to review its decision on any of the grounds referred to above, in which case the Secretary shall serve notice on the parties not later than 10 working days after the date on which the decision was sent to them, and the parties will have an opportunity to be heard.

36   If, as a result of his/her death or incapacity s/he is unable to sign, or if s/he ceases to be a member, it will be signed by another member of the Tribunal.

CHAPTER NINE

Staff Employment and Training

The employment and training of good staff lies at the heart of any successful care home. Regulations 18 and 19 of the Care Homes Regulations 2001 provide as follows:

Regulation 18: Staffing

The registered person must, having regard to the size of the care home, the statement of purpose and the number and needs of the residents, ensure that at all times suitably qualified, competent and experienced persons are working at the care home in such numbers as are appropriate for the health and welfare of residents. Where the care home provides nursing, medicines or medical treatment to residents, the registered provider must ensure that at all times a suitably qualified registered nurse is working at the care home. The employment of any persons on a temporary basis at the care home must not prevent residents from receiving such continuity of care as is reasonable to meet their needs. The registered person must ensure that persons working at the care home are appropriately trained and receive suitable assistance, including time off for the purpose of obtaining further appropriate qualifications. The registered person must make arrangements for providing persons who work at the care home with appropriate information about any Code of Practice published under the Care Standards Act 2000.

Regulation 19: Fitness of workers

The registered person must not employ a person to work at the care home unless the person is fit to work at the care home. This applies whether they are directly employed by the home, or indirectly, for example via an agency. The registered person must, in respect of each employee, be satisfied on reasonable grounds as to the person's identity, the authenticity of their qualifications so far as they are relevant to the work which that person is to perform at the care home, and the authenticity of their references. As part of this verification process, the registered person must have obtained copies of each of the above-mentioned documents, plus their birth certificate, their current passport (if any), a recent photograph of the person, a criminal record certificate, and if necessary, an enhanced criminal record certificate.[1] If the employee may, in the course of their duties, have regular contact with residents at the care home, the registered person must take extra precautions to satisfy themselves that the person is fit to work at the care home in this capacity, and in particular that they have qualifications suitable to the work that they are to perform, and the experience and skills necessary for such work, and also that they are physically and mentally fit to perform that work.

It is not the purpose of this chapter to set out in any detail the complex range of duties and responsibilities that employment law imposes upon employers in the selection, appointment, promotion, training and retention of their staff. A number of excellent specialist guides do this task more than adequately.[2] Rather, I have selected a few amongst a wide and miscellaneous range of recent changes in employment law that are likely to be of particular significance in the world of care homes. These areas are as follows:

1.   The training framework.

2.   Health and safety laws and regulations. (These are dealt with in Chapter Four)

3.   The national minimum wage.

4.   The rights of part-time workers.

5.   Whistleblowing.

6.   Maternity and Parental Leave Regulations.[3]

THE TRAINING FRAMEWORK

Regulation 18 of the Care Homes Regulations 2001 includes the following statement:

> The persons employed to work at the care home must receive training appropriate to the work they are to perform and suitable assistance, including time off for the purpose of obtaining further qualifications appropriate to such work.

Under the National Minimum Standards (Standard 28):

All staff must receive an induction training to TOPPS specification, within six weeks of appointment, plus foundation training to TOPPS specification within six months of appointment, equipping them to meet the assessed needs of residents as set out in their care plans. All staff must receive a further three paid days training a year, and have an individual training and development assessment and profile.

The training framework designed by TOPSS is divided into discrete sections and is comprehensive. They are all cast within the umbrella of the *Care Training Code*, issued by TOPSS in 2001 as 'a voluntary code of practice for trainers of social care students, candidates and staff and guide for purchasers of training'.[4]

Induction programme

This programme is designed to ensure that all new staff complete a training induction course before they work outside of close supervision by a fully inducted worker who takes responsibility for their practice, and in any event by the time they have been employed for six weeks.[5] The learning achieved in the induction programme counts towards NVQs in Care or related topics at Levels 2 and 3.[6] The training pack *Your Induction to Work in Social Care* can be obtained from TOPSS.[7]

Foundation standards

This programme follows the induction programme, and should normally be completed within the first six months of employment.[8] The Foundation Standards have been designed to enable care home staff to build on and develop the learning achieved by the induction programme. They require knowledge building, and its application in practice. They are linked to the overarching framework of the National Occupational Standards,[9] and form the basis for the NVQ qualifications required of care staff.[10]

There are five units in the Foundation Standards:

1. Understanding how to apply the value base of care.

2. Communicating effectively.

3. Developing as a worker.

4. Recognising and responding to abuse and neglect.

5. Understanding the experiences and particular needs of the individuals using the service.

Training for registered managers

TOPSS, in consultation with a large number of other bodies, has produced National Occupational Standards for Registered Managers in Health and Social Care.[11] National Occupational Standards have four purposes:

1.   They describe best practice in particular areas of work.

2.   They are statements of competence that combine the skills, knowledge and values necessary to undertake a work task.

3.   They provide a human resource management tool to assist in workforce management and supervision, quality control and specification of tasks.

4.   They provide a basis for training and assessment.

According to TOPSS, the National Occupational Standards for registered managers are 'likely to form the basis of a recognised national qualification of this group of staff in the future'.[12] At this stage, however, a softly-softly approach is being adopted towards existing care home managers, though this may change.

> Registered managers are an experienced group of professionals, many of whom already hold social care, nursing, social work or related qualifications. However the majority do not have a recognised management qualification. In future many registered managers will be in a position to access any new management qualification using Accreditation of Prior Experience and Learning Systems (APEL). These offer the opportunity to experienced people to compile a portfolio of evidence that demonstrates learning derived from practice. Credit towards all, or part, of the award could be claimed by the candidate. It is important to stress that there is no expectation that current competent managers would be required to undertake lengthy taught programmes leading to an award.[13]

The key words in this statement are probably 'lengthy' and 'taught'. It should *not* be assumed that managers in the future will not be expected to acquire a management qualification. Rather, at least in the short term, and for existing experienced managers, it should be relatively easy for them to obtain the management qualification that is appropriate to their role, on the basis of past experience, demonstrated by a portfolio.

The qualification, once it has been devised and accepted by the relevant curriculum authorities, and also approved by the General Social Care Council as the appropriate qualification for such work, is likely to be a mixture of core units demonstrating a range of basic management competences, and a range of more specialised optional units, from which the manager would select options appropriate to his/her particular work and skills. The level is NVQ Level 4.

Finally, note that TOPSS England has teamed up with recruitment publishers Care and Health to produce a training volume to help managers train their own staff through the new qualifications framework: *The First Six Months: A Registered Manager's Guide.*

For Health and Safety Laws and Regulations see Chapter Four at pp.72–3.[14]

NATIONAL MINIMUM WAGE

The National Minimum Wage Act 1998 (NMWA 1998) established a minimum hourly wage for workers, from 1 April 1999. Since October 2001, the rate has been set at £4.10 per hour for adult workers and £3.50 per hour for workers aged 18 to 21.[15]

A 'worker' is defined for these purposes as:[16]

> Someone working under a contract of employment or any other, under which an individual undertakes to do or perform in person any work or service for another.

The following do not qualify to receive the national minimum wage:[17]

- Those under 18 years of age.

- A worker under the age of 26 who is employed under a contract of apprenticeship and is in the first 12 months of that contract, or who has not reached the age of 19 years.

- A worker who is participating in a scheme designed to provide him or her with training work, or temporary work, or which is designed to assist him or her to obtain work.

- A worker who is attending higher education up to first degree level or a teacher-training course and has been placed in a care home for up to one year as part of their course. Postgraduate degree or diploma students do however qualify for the minimum wage.

- A homeless person who is provided with shelter and other benefits in return for performing work.

- A worker who works and lives in the employer's household as a member of the employer's family.

- Workers who are trainees on a government-funded training programme such as the New Deal, National Traineeships, or

Youth Training, unless they are workers employed by the employer for whom they work under the scheme (i.e. the residential home itself).

- Volunteers working for a charity, voluntary organisation, school or similar body, who receive only reasonable expenses or benefits in kind.

Special lower rates apply to workers aged over 22 who are in their first 6 months with an employer and are receiving at least 26 days of approved training during these 6 months.

The hourly rate is calculated by adding up the *total remuneration*, and dividing this figure by the total number of hours worked during a pay reference period (e.g. one month, or one week).[18]

No benefits in kind (e.g. meals) can be included as part of the national minimum wage, with the exception of accommodation, if it is supplied by the employer to the worker. This is however subject to a limit of either 50p for every hour of work in the pay reference period, or £2.85 for every day accommodation is provided in the pay reference period, whichever is the lower (and subject in any event to a maximum offset of £19.95 per week).

Total remuneration is calculated by adding together:

- all monies paid by the employer to the worker during the reference period;

- any money paid by the employer to the worker in the following reference period which is in respect of work done in the current reference period;

- any money paid by the employer to the worker later than the end of the following pay reference period in respect of work done in the current reference period and for which the worker is under an obligation to complete a record and has not done so;

- the cost of accommodation, calculated by an approved formula.

If workers in any of the categories that entitle them to the national minimum wage are on standby or call at or near the residential home, they must be paid at least the national minimum wage.

There are also some periods of travel time when the national minimum wage must be paid. The most significant are:

- travelling in connection with work during normal working hours, but not including time travelling to and from work;

- travelling to a place of training during normal working hours;

- waiting to collect goods, to meet someone in connection with work, or to start a job in connection with work.

If workers arrange with their employers to sleep at their place of work from time to time, this 'sleeping time' will not be treated as qualifying for the national minimum wage, unless they have to get up and do some work in the night, which time they will be paid for.

THE RIGHTS OF PART-TIME EMPLOYEES

Although part-time employees have traditionally been less favourably treated in their conditions of employment than full-time staff, especially in relation to pay, holidays and non-pay benefits, recent changes in European Union Law are starting to redress this imbalance. The Employment Relations Act 1999 and the Part Time Workers (Prevention of Less Favourable Treatment) Regulations 2000 ('the Regulations'),[19] contain the key changes in this regard.

The new regime applies to all employers who employ both full-time and part-time staff. Unlike under the Disability Discrimination Act 1995, there is no exception for small businesses. Under the legislation, a worker is either 'an individual who works under a contract of employment (an "employee")' or 'an individual who agrees personally to provide any work or services for another, provided the person for whom the work is done is not a client or customer of any business carried on by the individual'. This means that effectively all employees serving under a contract of employment are protected by the Regulations, including those workers who are not strictly employees in the narrow sense (e.g. agency workers) but who normally work for one employer.

The distinction between who is a full-time employee and who is a part-time employee is a vital one. Part-time employees making a claim under the Regulations must establish that they are being treated less favourably than comparable full-time employees. The person with whom the part-time employee chooses to compare him/herself (his/her 'comparator') must therefore be drawn from the pool of full-timers. A full-time employee is one who, under the normal, working arrangements of that particular employer, is regarded as full-time.[20] A part-time employee is someone who works for less than the normal full-time hours. Only part-time workers acquire rights under the Regulations. [21]

If employees become part-time, having been full-time, or if they take leave of absence and return part-time after leave of less than 12 months, they retain the right not to be treated less favourably than they were treated before going part-time with the same employer. As employees who seek to make such changes need to be protected against less favourable treatment after they cease to work full-time, the usual comparison does not apply. In these circumstances the comparison to be made is between the individual work circumstances when they were full-time, and their circumstances when becoming part-time. For these purposes there is deemed to be a full-time worker employed on the terms on which the worker was employed before the change or leave of absence, even if this is not actually the case.

Who is the comparator?

A full-time employee is a suitable comparator, if at the time when the less favourable treatment allegedly takes place, both employees are:

- employed by the employer under 'the same type of contract'; *and*
- engaged in the same, or broadly similar work having regard, where relevant, to whether they have a similar level of qualifications, skills and experience.[22]

The comparator must be based at the same care home as the part-time worker, unless no full-timer's work at that home fulfils the above criteria. In such a case the comparator can be a full-time employee at another care home of the same employer who does fulfil those criteria.

What rights do part-time employees have?

The basic right conferred on a part-time employee is a right not to be treated by the employer less favourably than a full-time employee, either in relation to any term of the contract (this will prevent discrimination in relation to both express and implied terms), or by being subjected to any other detriment by any act, or any deliberate failure to act, of his/her employer.[23] These rights are, however, subject to limitations. For example, a part-time employee who works fewer hours than a comparable full-time employee will earn less in take home pay, but is not treated less favourably if the *rate of pay* per hour is the same. If it is not the same rate of pay the difference must be objectively justified.

Justification means the employer can show that the difference in pay or conditions occurs to achieve a genuine business objective, that the difference is necessary and also that the difference is appropriate to achieve that objective. In providing an objective evaluation of his/her practices it is not enough for the employer to believe that there were good reasons for discriminating. It requires an objective assessment of whether the reasons are sufficient and that the difference in pay or conditions is an appropriate means of achieving the employer's business objectives. Measuring the benefit to the employer and the disadvantage to the employee is normally a relevant factor. This is because the advantage to the employer must be proportionate to the harm suffered by the individual.

A further limitation relates to overtime payments. Part-time employees are not entitled to payment at overtime rates merely because they work beyond their own normal contracted hours. A legal right to an overtime payment only arises where part-time employees have worked beyond the normal hours of comparable full-time employees.[24]

Making a claim for compensation

If part-time employees believe that they are being treated less favourably than a comparable full-timer, the first step is to request a written statement of the reasons for this treatment.[25] The written statements are admissible as evidence in a claim brought before an Employment Tribunal. If the employee wishes then to take his/her employer to the Employment Tribunal s/he must issue proceedings within three months from the date, or last date, on which the less favourable treatment occurred. If the employee is successful at the hearing the Employment Tribunal can make a declaration of the rights of the part-time worker and of the employer respectively, and also, if it is thought appropriate, it can order the employer to compensate the part-time employee.

WHISTLEBLOWING

The Public Interest Disclosure Act 1998 protects individuals, in certain specified situations, from victimisation or other adverse treatment, for making a disclosure ('blowing the whistle') to their employer, or other responsible person (for example the National Care Standards Commission or the Social Services Inspectorate (SSI)), about something they reasonably believe tends to show any of the following, where such disclosure is in the public interest (described as as 'qualifying disclosure'):

- a criminal offence;
- a failure to comply with any legal obligation;
- a miscarriage of justice;
- danger to the health and safety of *any individual* (i.e. not necessarily a worker);
- damage to the environment;
- the deliberate concealment of information tending to expose any of the above.

It is automatically unfair to dismiss a worker for making a qualifying disclosure. The worker must however show that s/he acted honestly and in good faith, in reporting the alleged misdemeanour.

A number of decided cases demonstrate the general parameters in which 'whistleblowing' will be protected. In *Stephens v Englishcombe House Residential Home*,[26] a complaint to management by a night supervisor that medical treatment had not been properly administered was deemed to be a qualifying disclosure on the grounds of health and safety; in *Chattenton v City of Sunderland City Council*,[27] reporting that pornographic images had been found on an office computer was deemed to be a qualifying disclosure, as the employee believed that a criminal offence may have occurred. In *Boughton v National Tyre Ltd*[28] an employee reported to a senior manager what he reasonably and genuinely believed to have been a criminal offence in the workplace. The senior manager failed to investigate the information, or show support for the employee, and the Employment Tribunal held that in the circumstances the employee could consider himself to have been constructively (and unfairly) dismissed, and entitled to compensation. Finally, the case of *Bladon v ALM Medical Services Ltd*,[29] is worthy of special consideration. Bladon reported adversely on the standard of patient care in the home where he worked, to the managing director's PA. This was deemed to be a qualifying disclosure to his employer. He then reported his concerns to the SSI on the grounds that the information was of a serious nature. The SSI was an appropriate investigatory body, and his employer did not have a whistleblowing procedure. He was dismissed for his efforts. The Employment Tribunal found the dismissal to be automatically unfair, and awarded him £23,000 compensation.[30]

It remains an open question whether or not an employee has a *legal duty* to report activities that fall into any of the above categories. This could become an important issue, if as a result of the failure to report some observed ill-treatment the victim suffers damage or injury.

MATERNITY AND PARENTAL LEAVE REGULATIONS 1999[31]

These Regulations set out a series of employee rights to maternity and paternity leave. Every person who cares for a young child, or who has recently adopted a child, has the right to take time off from his/her employment to care for that child.[32] To be eligible for leave, the employee must have one year of continuous employment at the date the leave is due to start. The entitlement is to 13 weeks of leave.[33] Part-time employees will be entitled to leave commensurate with the time worked, e.g. a person who works 2 days a week will be entitled to two-fifths of 13 weeks. Leave can be taken up to a child's fifth birthday, or fifth anniversary of adoption, or the 18th birthday of a child entitled to a disability living allowance.[34]

Whilst employers are not entitled to refuse leave, they can postpone[35] leave for a period of up to six months, so long as they give notice of the postponement at least two weeks before the leave was due to start, and the operation of the business would be unduly disrupted if the employee took leave during the period identified in his/her notice.

Employees have a right to return to the same job that they left, unless it is not reasonably practicable for the employer to allow them to do so. If this is the case, they can be allocated to another job, providing that it is suitable and appropriate.

ENDNOTES

1   This will be required if the position falls under s.115 (4) of the Police Act 1997, and s.90 CSA 2000. It is part of the process whereby records are kept regarding people considered 'unsuitable to work with vulnerable adults', under s.81 CSA. On criminal convictions and employment in care homes see Chapter Two at p.24.

2   Lewis and Sargeant (2000) *Essentials of Employment Law,* Institute of Personnel and Development is one recommended example.

3   Annex to Parental Leave Directive No. 96/34/EC, extended to the United Kingdom by Council Directive 97/75/EC.

4   This together with all the TOPSS documentation can be obtained from the TOPSS website, www.TOPSS.org.uk, or direct from TOPSS England, 26 Park Row, Leeds, LS1 5QB

5   *Your Induction to Work in Social Care, p.2.* TOPSS England.

6   *Your Induction to Work in Social Care,* p.3. TOPSS England.

7   TOPSS England, 26 Park Row, Leeds, LS1 5QB, Tel: 0113 245 6417. See also TOPSS Wales, Tel: 029 2022 6257; TOPSS Scotland, Tel: 0131 244 1949; TOPSS Northern Ireland, Tel: 028 9066 5390.

8   *The TOPSS England Foundation Standards 2001–2,* TOPSS 2001, p.1.

9   See Chapter One at p.17.

10   See Chapter One at p.17.

11   See www.topss.org.uk

12   Introduction to the Working Draft of the NOSRM-Adult Care Homes, TOPSS 2000, 5.1.

13   Introduction to the Working Draft of the NOSRM-Adult Care Homes, TOPSS 2001, 5.1.

14   See also the NCHA booklet *Health and Safety in Residential and Nursing Homes at Work* (Produced annually, cost £1. Designed essentially for employees. NCHA also produce a large manual, which is considerably more expensive.); and Health and Safety in Care Homes, HSEG 220, HSE Books 2001.

15   National Minimum Wage Regulations 1999 (Amendment) (No. 2) Regulations 2001 SI No. 2673.
16   NMWA 1998 s.54(3).
17   National Minimum Wage Regulations 1999, Regulation 12.
18   National Minimum Wage Regulations 1999, Regulations 10, 14.
19   SI 2000, No. 1551, implementing the EU Directive on Part-Time Work (Council Directive 97/81/EC).
20   Regulation 2.
21   Regulation 2.
22   Regulation 2 (4).
23   Regulation 5.
24   Regulation 5 (4).
25   Regulation 6.
26   Case 5301067/00.
27   Case 6402938/99.
28   Case 1500080/00.
29   Case 2405845/99.
30   The case of *Fernandes v Netcom Consultants Ltd* (Case 2200060/00) has made the highest compensation award to date for dismissal following qualifying disclosure, namely £293,441! This exceptionally high figure was due to the fact that the applicant had lost his job at 58, and it was thought unlikely that he would find further employment.
31   SI 1999, No. 3312.
32   Regulation 13 (1).
33   Regulation 14.
34   Regulation 15.
35   Regulations Schedule 2. s.6.

Glossary of Key Terms

Registered Manager
A person who is registered under Part II of the Care Standards Act as the manager of the care home.

Registered Person
Any person who is the registered provider or registered manager in respect of the care home.

Registered Provider
A person who is registered under Part II of the Care Standards Act as a person carrying on the care home. In the case of a local authority home, it is for the local authority to decide who this person should be.

Relative
(in relation to any person) this can be:

    (a) the person's spouse;

    (b) any lineal ancestor, lineal descendant, brother, sister, uncle, aunt, nephew or niece of his or his spouse;

    (c) the spouse of any relative within sub-paragraph (b) of this definition, and for the purpose of determining any such relationship a person's step-child shall be treated as his/her child, and references to 'spouse' include a former spouse and a person who is living with the person as a husband or wife.

Representative
In relation to a service user, a person, other than the registered person or a person employed at the care home, who with the service user's express or implied consent takes an interest in the service user's health and welfare.

Responsible Individual

The person in the care home who is a director, manager, secretary, or other officer of the organisation and who is responsible for supervising the management of the care home.

Service User

Any person in the care home who is in need of nursing or personal care by reason of disability, infirmity, past or present illness, past or present mental disorder or past or present dependence on alcohol or drugs.

Staff

Persons employed by the registered person to work at the care home, but does not include a volunteer or a person employed under a contract for services.

Statement of Purpose

The written statement compiled in accordance with Registration Regulation 4 (1).

Department of Health

The National Care Standards Commission (Registration) Regulations 2001

PART II – APPLICATIONS FOR REGISTRATION

Information and documents to be provided by an applicant

3. (1) An application for registration shall –

  (a) be in writing on a form approved by the Commission;

  (b) be sent or delivered to the Commission;

  (c) be accompanied by a recent photograph of the responsible person, of whom the photograph shall be a true likeness;

  (d) give the information that the applicant is required to provide in accordance with paragraphs (2) to (4).

(2) A person who is seeking to be registered as a person who carries on an establishment or agency shall provide to the Commission –

  (a) full information in respect of each of the matters listed in Parts I and II of Schedule 1;

  (b) the documents listed in paragraphs 1 to 3 and 5 to 9 of Schedule 2.

  (c) the documents listed in paragraphs 4 and 10 of Schedule 2, except where any certificate or information on any matters referred to in those paragraphs is not available to an individual because any provision of the Police Act 1997 has not been brought into force.

(3) A person who is seeking to be registered as a manager in respect of an establishment or agency shall provide to the Commission –

  (a) full information in respect of each of the matters listed in Part I of Schedule 3;

  (b) the documents listed in paragraphs 9 to 11 of that Schedule.

  (c) the documents listed in paragraphs 12 and 13 of that Schedule, except where any certificate ot information on any matters referred to in those paragraphs is not available to the person because any provision of the Police Act 1997 has not been brought into force.

(4) A person who is seeking to be registered in respect of an establishment or agency of a description specified in column (1) below shall provide to the Commission full information in respect of each of the matters listed in the Schedule specified in the corresponding entry in column (2) below.

(1) Establishment or agency	(2) Schedule
Care home	Schedule 4
Children's home	Schedule 5
Independent hospital, independent clinic, or independent medical agency	Schedule 6

(5) If the Commission so requests, the applicant shall provide full information to the Commission in respect of the matters listed in Part III of Schedule 1 in relation to any person specified for this purpose by the Commission who works, or is intended to work, at the establishment or for the purposes of the agency.

(6) The applicant shall provide to the Commission any other information or documents that it may reasonably require in relation to his application for registration.

Convictions

4.   Where the Commission asks the responsible person for details of any criminal convictions which are spent within the meaning of section 1 of the Rehabilitation of Offenders Act 1974 and informs him at the time the question is asked that by virtue of the Rehabilitation of Offenders Act 1974 (Exceptions) Order 1975 spent convictions are to be disclosed, he shall supply in writing to the Commission details of any spent convictions that he has.

Interview

5.   The responsible person shall attend an interview for the purpose of enabling the Commission to determine whether the applicant is fit to carry on or manage the establishment or agency in respect of which the applicant seeks to be registered.

Notice of changes

6.   The applicant shall give notice in writing to the Commission of any change specified below which occurs after the application for registration is made and before it is determined –

(a)   any change of the name or address of the applicant or any responsible person;

(b)   where the applicant is a partnership, any change of membership of the partnership;

(c)   where the applicant is an organisation, any change of director, manager, secretary or other person responsible for the management of the organisation.

Information as to staff engaged after application made

7.   (1) Where an applicant applies for registration as a person who carries on an establishment or agency, and before the application is determined, engages a person to work at the establishment or for the purposes of the agency, he shall, in respect of each person so engaged –

(a)   obtain the information specified in paragraphs 16 and 17 of Schedule 1 and, except where paragraph (2) applies, the documents specified in paragraph 10 of Schedule 2, in relation to the position in which the person is to work;

(b)   provide to the Commission, if it so requests, any of the information or documents which he is required to obtain under paragraph (a).

(2) This paragraph applies where any certificate or information on any matters referred to in paragraph 10 of Schedule 2 is not available to an individual because any provision of the Police Act 1997 has not been brought into force.

PART III – CERTIFICATES OF REGISTRATION

Registers

8.   (1) The Commission shall keep a register in respect of each description of establishment or agency specified in section 4(8)(a) or (9)(a) of the Act, other than that of voluntary adoption agency.

(2) Each register shall contain, in relation to each establishment or agency in respect of which a person's application for registration has been granted –

(a)   the particulars specified in Part I of Schedule 7; and

(b)   the particulars specified in respect of the register in Part II of that Schedule.

Contents of certificate

9.   Where the Commission is required to issue a certificate of registration it shall ensure that the certificate contains the following particulars –

(a)   the name, address and telephone number of the Commission;

(b)   the name and address of the person who has been registered as the person who carries on the establishment of agency;

(c) where the person is an organisation, the name of the responsible individual;

(d) the name of the person registered as the manager of the establishment or agency;

(e) the description of the establishment or agency by reference to the description of establishment or agency specified in section 4(8)(a) or (9)(a) of the Act;

(f) where the registration is subject to any condition, details of the condition including any requirement in the condition as to –

  (i) the facilities or services that are to be provided;

  (ii) the number of service users for whom accommodation or services may be provided;

  (iii) the description of persons to whom facilities or services are to be provided;

  (iv) any period of time within which the condition is to be fulfilled;

  (v) the number and description of persons to be working at any specified place and time;

(g) the date of registration;

(h) a statement that if an establishment or agency is not carried on in accordance with the relevant requirements and conditions the registration is liable to be cancelled by the Commission;

(i) a statement that the certificate relates only to the person to whom it is issued by the Commission and is not capable of being transferred to another person.

Return of certificate

10. If the registration of a person in respect of an establishment or agency is cancelled, he shall, not later than the day on which the decision or order cancelling the registration takes effect, return the certificate of registration to the Commission by –

(a) delivering it to the Commission; or

(b) sending it to the Commission by registered post or by recorded delivery.

Offence

11. (1) A failure to comply with regulation 10 shall be an offence.

(2) The Commission shall not bring proceedings against a person in respect of any failure to comply with that regulation unless –

(a) notice has been given to him in accordance with paragraph (3);

(b) the period specified in the notice, beginning with the date of the notice, has expired; and

(c)   the person fails to comply with that regulation.

(3) Where the Commission considers that the person has failed to comply with regulation 10, it may serve a notice on the person specifying –

(a)   in what respect in its opinion the person has failed or is failing to comply with the requirements of that regulation;

(b)   what action, in the opinion of the Commission, the person should take so as to comply with that regulation; and

(c)   the period, not exceeding three months, within which the person should take action.

PART IV – CONDITIONS AND REPORTS

Application for variation or removal of a condition

12.   (1) In this regulation –

"application" means an application by the registered person under section 15(1)(a) of the Act for the variation or removal of a condition in relation to his registration;

"proposed effective date" means the date requested by the registered person as the date on which the variation or removal applied for is to take effect.

(2) An application shall be –

(a)   made in writing on a form approved by the Commission;

(b)   sent or delivered to the Commission not less than three months before the proposed effective date or such shorter period (if any) before that date as may be agreed with the Commission;

(c)   accompanied by the information specified in paragraph (3);

(d)   accompanied by a fee of such amount as may be prescribed in relation to the variation or removal applied for by any regulation made under section 15(3) of the Act.

(3) The following information is specified –

(a)   the proposed effective date;

(b)   the registered person's reasons for making the application;

(c)   details of changes that the registered person proposes to make in relation to the establishment or agency as a consequence of the variation or removal applied for, including details of –

(i)   proposed structural changes to the premises that are used as an establishment or for the purposes of an agency;

>   (ii)   additional staff, facilities or equipment, or changes in management that are required to ensure that the proposed changes are carried into effect.

(4) The registered person shall provide the Commission with any other information or any documents that it may reasonably require in relation to his application.

Report as to financial viability

13. If it appears to the registered person that the establishment or agency is likely to cease to be financially viable at any time within the next following six months, the registered person shall give a report to the Commission of the relevant circumstances.

PART V – CANCELLATION OF REGISTRATION

Cancellation of registration

14. The following grounds are specified for the purposes of section 14(1)(d) of the Act as grounds on which the Commission may cancel the registration of a person in respect of an establishment or agency –

(a)   he has failed to pay at the time prescribed under subsection (3) of section 16 of the Act the annual fee payable by him by virtue of that subsection;

(b)   he has in relation to any application by him –

>   (i)   for registration; or
>
>   (ii)   for the variation or removal of a condition in relation to his registration,
>
> made a statement which is false or misleading in a material respect or provided false information;

(c)   the establishment or agency has ceased to be financially viable, or is likely to cease to be so within the next six months.

Application for cancellation of registration

15. (1) In this regulation –

"application for cancellation" means an application by the registered person under section 15(1)(b) of the Act for the cancellation of his registration;

"notice of application for cancellation" means a notice by the registered person stating that he has made, or intends to make, an application for cancellation;

"proposed effective date" means the date requested by the registered person as the date on which the cancellation applied for is to take effect.

(2) An application for cancellation shall be –

    (a)   made in writing on a form approved by the Commission;

    (b)   sent or delivered to the Commission not less than three months before the proposed effective date or such shorter period (if any) before that date as may be agreed with the Commission;

    (c)   accompanied by the information specified in paragraph (4).

(3) If the registered person makes an application for cancellation he shall not more than seven days thereafter give notice of application for cancellation to each of the persons specified in paragraph (4)(d), other than a person to whom he has given such notice within three months before he made the application for cancellation.

(4) The following information is specified –

    (a)   the proposed effective date;

    (b)   a statement as to the arrangements (if any) that have been made by the registered person to ensure that on and after –

        (i)   the date of application for cancellation; and

        (ii)   the proposed effective date,

        service users will continue to be provided with similar accommodation (if any) and services as those provided to them in the establishment or by the agency at the date on which the application for cancellation is made;

    (c)   the registered person's reasons for making the application for cancellation;

    (d)   particulars of any notice of application for cancellation that has been given to any of the following persons –

        (i)   service users;

        (ii)   persons who appear to the registered person to be representatives of service users;

        (iii)   the local authority and Health Authority in whose areas the establishment or the premises used by the agency are situated;

    (e)   where the registered person has not given notice of application for cancellation to –

        (i)   each service user;

        (ii)   in respect of each service user, a person who appears to the registered person to be a representative of that service user; and

        (iii)   each of the bodies specified in sub-paragraph (4)(d)(iii), a statement as to whether there were any circumstances which prevented the registered person from giving, or made it impracticable for him to give, notice of application for cancellation to any of the persons or bodies referred to in heads (i) to (iii) of this sub-paragraph before the date on which he applied for cancellation.

(f) where the registered person has applied for cancellation less than three months before the proposed effective date, a report as to whether the establishment or agency has ceased, or is likely to cease within the next following twelve months, to be financially viable.

(5) The registered person shall provide the Commission with any other information or any documents that it may reasonably require in relation to his application for cancellation.

SCHEDULE 1 Regulation 3(2)(a) and (5)

INFORMATION TO BE SUPPLIED ON AN APPLICATION FOR REGISTRATION AS A PERSON WHO CARRIES ON AN ESTABLISHMENT OR AGENCY

PART I

Information about the applicant

1. Where the applicant is an individual –

   (a) if he intends to carry on the establishment or agency in partnership with others, the information specified in the following sub-paragraphs of this paragraph in relation to each partner of the firm;

   (b) the responsible person's full name, date of birth, address and telephone number;

   (c) details of his professional or technical qualifications, and experience of carrying on an establishment or agency, so far as such qualifications and experience are relevant to providing services for persons to whom services are to be provided at the establishment or by the agency;

   (d) details of his employment history, including the name and address of his present employer and of any previous employers;

   (e) details of any business the person carries on or has carried on;

   (f) the name and addresses of two referees –

      (i) who are not relatives of the responsible person;

      (ii) each of whom is able to provide a reference as to the responsible person's competence to carry on an establishment or agency of the same description as the establishment or agency; and

(iii)   one of whom has employed the responsible person for a period of at least 3 months,

but the requirement for the name and address of a referee who has employed the applicant for a period of at least 3 months shall not apply where it is impracticable to obtain a reference from a person who fulfils that requirement;

(g)   where any certificate or information on any matters referred to in paragraph 4 of Schedule 2 is not available to the responsible person because any provision of the Police Act 1997 has not been brought into force, details of any criminal offences –

(i)   of which the responsible person has been convicted, including details of any convictions which are spent within the meaning of section I of the Rehabilitation of Offenders Act 1974 and which may be disclosed by virtue of the Rehabilitation of Offenders Act 1974 (Exceptions) Order 1975; or

(ii)   in respect of which he has been cautioned by a constable and which, at the time the caution was given, he admitted.

2.   Where the applicant is a partnership –

(a)   the name and address of the partnership;

(b)   in relation to each member of the partnership, the information specified in paragraph 1 (b) to (h).

3.   Where the applicant is an organisation –

(a)   the name of the organisation and the address of the registered office or principal office of the organisation;

(b)   the full name, date of birth, address and telephone number of the responsible individual;

(c)   details of the professional or technical qualifications of the responsible individual and his experience of carrying on an establishment or agency of the same description as the establishment or agency, so far as such qualifications and experience are relevant to providing services for persons for whom services are to be provided at the establishment or by the agency;

(d)   if the organisation is a subsidiary of a holding company, the name and address of the registered or principal office of the holding company and of any other subsidiary of that holding company.

4.   In every case –

(a)   a reference from a bank expressing an opinion as to the registered provider's financial standing;

(b)   a statement as to whether the responsible person has been adjudged bankrupt, or sequestration of his estate has been ordered, or he has made a composition or arrangement with, or granted a trust deed for, his creditors;

(c)   a statement as to the applicant's ability to ensure the financial viability of the establishment or agency for the purpose of achieving the aims and objectives of the establishment or agency set out in its statement of purpose;

(d)   a business plan in respect of the establishment or agency;

(e)   details as to cash-flow in respect of the establishment or agency.

PART II

Information about the establishment or agency

5.   The name, address, telephone number, facsimile number, and electronic mail address (if any) of the establishment or agency.

6.   The description of establishment or agency specified in section 4(8)(a) or (9)(a) of the Act in respect of which the applicant seeks to be registered.

7.   The statement of purpose of the establishment or agency.

8.   A statement as to the accommodation, facilities and services which are to be provided by the establishment or agency including the extent and, where appropriate, location of such accommodation, facilities and services.

9.   The date on which the establishment or agency was established or is proposed to be established.

10.   Details of the scale of charges payable by the service users.

11.   In respect of the premises to be used by an establishment –

(a)   a description of the premises, including a statement as to whether the premises are purpose-built or have been converted for use an establishment;

(b)   a description of the area in which the premises are located.

12.   In respect of the premises to be used by an establishment or for the purposes of an agency, a statement as to whether at the date the application is made the premises are capable of being used for the purpose of –

(a)   achieving the aims and objectives set out in the statement of purpose of the establishment or agency; and

(b)   providing facilities and services in accordance with the statement referred to in paragraph 8,

without the need for planning permission, building works, or conversion of the premises and, if the premises are not capable of such use at the date the application is made, details of the permission, works or conversion needed.

13.   A statement as to the security arrangements, including arrangements for the purposes of –

(a)   safeguarding access to information held by the establishment or agency; and

(b)   restricting access from adjacent premises or, when the premises form part of a building, from other parts of the building.

14.   The name and address of any other establishment or agency of a description specified in section 4(8)(a) or (9)(a) of the Act in which the applicant has or has had a business or financial interest, or at which he is or has been employed, and details of such interest or employment.

15.   Whether any other business is or will be carried on in the same premises as those of the establishment or agency and, if so, details of such business.

Information about staff

16.   In respect of any person, other than the applicant, who works at, or is intended to work at the establishment or for the agency –

(a)   the person's name, sex and date of birth;

(b)   the person's duties and responsibilities in relation to his work.

PART III

Further information about staff

17.   In respect of any person, other than the applicant, who works at, or is intended to work at the establishment or for the purposes of the agency-

(a)   whether the person is, or is intended to be, resident in the premises used as the establishment or for the purposes of the agency;

(b)   if he is a relative of any person who has made an application in respect of the establishment or agency, his relationship to such person;

(c)   whether the person works or is intended to work, on a full-time basis or on a part-time basis and, if on a part-time basis, the number of hours per week for which it is intended that the person will work;

(d)   the date on which the person commenced, or is intended to commence, working at the establishment or for the purposes of the agency;

(e)   information as to the person's qualifications, experience and skills in so far as is relevant to the work that the person is to perform;

(f)   a statement by applicant that he is satisfied as to the authenticity of the qualifications, and has verified the experience and skills that are referred in sub-paragraph (e);

(g)   a statement as to –

(i)   the suitability of the person's qualifications for the work that the person is to perform;

(ii)   whether the person has the skills necessary for such work;

(iii)   the person's fitness to work, and have regular contact, with service users;

(h)   a statement by the person as to the state of his physical and mental health;

(i)   a statement by the applicant that the person is physically and mentally fit for the purposes of the work which he is to perform;

(j)   a statement by the applicant as to whether he is satisfied as to the person's identity, the means by which he so satisfied himself and whether he has obtained a copy of the person's birth certificate;

(k)   confirmation by the applicant that he has a recent photograph of the person;

(l)   a statement by the applicant that he has obtained two references relating to the person and that he is satisfied as to the authenticity of those references;

(m)   details of any criminal offences of which the person has been convicted, including details of any convictions which are spent within the meaninfg of section 1 of the Rehabilitation of Offenders Act 1974 and which may be disclosed by virtue of the Rehabilitation of Offenders Act 1974 (Exceptions) Order 1975, and, in relation to each offence, a statement by the person –

(i)   as to whether in his view the conviction is relevant to his suitability to care for, train, supervise or be in sole charge of any person and, if so,

(ii)   as to why he considers that he is suitable to perform the work in which he is to be employed;

(n)   details of any criminal offences in respect of which he has been cautioned by a constable and which, at the time the caution was given, he admitted.

SCHEDULE 2 Regulation 3(2)(b)

DOCUMENTS TO BE SUPPLIED ON AN APPLICATION FOR REGISTRATION AS A PERSON WHO CARRIES ON AN ESTABLISHMENT OR AGENCY

Documents concerning applicant

1.   The responsible person's birth certificate.

2.   Certificates or other suitable evidence relating to the responsible person's professional or technical qualifications, so far as such qualifications are relevant to providing services for persons for whom services are to be provided at the establishment or by the agency.

3. (1) Subject to sub-paragraph (2), a report by a general medical practitioner as to whether the responsible person is physically and mentally fit to carry on an establishment or agency of the same description as the establishment or agency.

    (2) Where the responsible person is unable to obtain the report referred to in sub-paragraph (1), a statement by the responsible person as to the state of his physical and mental health.

4. The following documents in relation to the responsible person –

    (a) a criminal record certificate –

        (i)   which has been issued under section 113 of the Police Act 1997; and

        (ii) the application for which was countersigned by the Commission,

        including, where applicable, the matters specified in section 113(3A)(a) and (b) and (3C)(a) and (b) of that Act;

    (b) an enhanced criminal record certificate –

        (i)   which has been issued under section 115 of that Act; and

        (ii) the application for which was countersigned by the Commission,

        including, where applicable, the matters specified in section 115(6A)(a) and (b) and (6B)(a) and (b) of that Act.

5. Where the applicant is a corporate body, a copy of each of its last two annual reports.

6. Where the organisation is a subsidiary of a holding company, the name and address of the registered or principal office and the last two annual reports (if any) of the holding company and of any other subsidiary of that holding company.

7. The last annual accounts (if any) of the establishment or agency.

8. Except where the applicant is a local authority or NHS trust, a reference from a bank expressing an opinion as to the applicant's financial standing.

9. A certificate of insurance for the applicant in respect of liability which may be incurred by him in relation to the establishment or agency in respect of death, injury, public liability, damage or other loss.

Criminal record certificates in respect of staff

10. (1) A statement confirming that –

    (a) the documents specified in sub-paragraph (2) have been issued –

        (i)   in the case of any applicant, to every person, other than the applicant, who works, or is intended to work, for the purposes of the establishment or agency; and

        (ii) where the applicant is an organisation, to the responsible individual; and

(b)   the applicant will make the documents so issued available for inspection by the Commission if the Commission so requires.

(2) The following documents are specified –

(a)   if the position in which the person works, or is intended to work, for the purposes of the establishment or agency falls within section 113(3B) of the Police Act 1997, either –

(i)   if the position falls within section 115(3) of that Act, an enhanced criminal record certificate issued to the person under section 115 of that Act; or

(ii)   in any other case, a criminal record certificate issued to the person under section 113 of that Act,

including the matters specified in, as the case may be, section 115(6A)(a) and (b) or 113(3A)(a) and (b) of that Act;

(b)   if the position in which the person works, or is intended to work, for the purposes of the establishment or agency falls within section 113(3D) of the Police Act 1997, either –

(i)   if the position falls within section 115(4) of that Act, an enhanced criminal record certificate issued to the person under section 115 of that Act; or

(ii)   in any other case, a criminal record certificate issued to the person under section 113 of that Act,

including the matters specified in, as the case may be, section 115(6B)(a) and (b) or 113(3C)(a) and (b) of that Act;

(c)   if the position in which the person works, or is intended to work, for the purposes of the establishment or agency does not fall within section 113(3B) or (3D) of the Police Act 1997, a criminal record certificate issued to the person under section 113 of that Act.

SCHEDULE 3 Regulation 3(3)

INFORMATION AND DOCUMENTS TO BE SUPPLIED ON AN APPLICATION FOR REGISTRATION AS THE MANAGER OF AN ESTABLISHMENT OR AGENCY

PART I

Information

1.   The applicant's full name, date of birth, address and telephone number.

2.   Details of the applicant's professional or technical qualifications, and experience of managing an establishment or agency, so far as such qualifications and experience are relevant to providing services for persons for whom services are to be provided at the establishment or by the agency.

3.   Details of the applicant's professional training relevant to carrying on or managing an establishment or agency.

4.   Details of the applicant's employment history, including the name and address of his present employer and of any previous employers.

5.   Details of any business the applicant carries on or manages or has carried on or managed.

6.   The name and addresses of two referees –

   (a)   who are not relatives of the applicant;

   (b)   each of whom is able to provide a reference as to the applicant's competence to carry on an establishment or agency of the same description as the establishment or agency; and

   (c)   one of whom has employed the applicant for a period of at least 3 months,

   but the requirement for the name and address of a referee who has employed the applicant for a period of at least 3 months shall not apply where it is impracticable to obtain a reference from a person who fulfils that requirement.

7.   The name, address, telephone number, facsimile number, and electronic mail address (if any) of the establishment or agency.

8.   Where any certificate or information on any matters referred to in paragraph 12 or 13 is not available to the applicant because any provision of the Police Act 1997 has not been brought into force, details of any criminal offences –

   (i)   of which the applicant has been convicted, including details of any convictions which are spent within the meaning of section 1 of the Rehabilitation of Offenders Act 1974 and which may be disclosed by virtue of the Rehabilitation of Offenders Act 1974 (Exceptions) Order 1975; or

   (ii)   in respect of which he has been cautioned by a constable and which, at the time the caution was given, he admitted.

PART II

Documents

9.   The applicant's birth certificate.

10.   Certificates or other suitable evidence relating to the applicant's professional or technical qualifications, so far as such qualifications are relevant to providing

services for persons for whom services are to be provided at the establishment or by the agency.

11. A report by a general medical practitioner as to whether the applicant is physically and mentally fit to manage an establishment or agency of the same description as the establishment or agency.

(1) Subject to sub-paragraph (2), a report by a general medical practitioner as to whether the applicant is physically and mentally fit to carry on an establishment or agency of the same description as the establishment or agency.

(2) Where the applicant is unable to obtain the report referred to in sub-paragraph (1), a statement by the applicant as to the state of his physical and mental health.

12. A criminal record certificate –

(a) which has been issued to the applicant under section 113 of the Police Act 1997; and

(b) the application for which was countersigned by the Commission,

including, where applicable, the matters specified in section 113(3A)(a) and (b) and (3C)(a) and (b) of that Act.

13. An enhanced criminal record certificate –

(a) which has been issued to the applicant under section 115 of that Act; and

(b) the application for which was countersigned by the Commission,

including, where applicable, the matters specified in section 115(6A)(a) and (b) and (6B)(a) and (b) of that Act.

SCHEDULE 4 Regulation 3(4)

INFORMATION TO BE SUPPLIED ON AN APPLICATION
FOR REGISTRATION IN RESPECT OF A CARE HOME

1. In this Schedule "service user" means any person in the care home who is in need of nursing or personal care by reason of disability, infirmity, past or present illness, past or present mental disorder or past or present dependence on alcohol or drugs.

2. Details of the accommodation available for –

(a) service users; and

(b) persons working at the care home.

3. Whether it is proposed to provide nursing at the care home.

4.   Whether it is proposed to provide at the care home accommodation, nursing or personal care to service users who are children.

5.   The maximum number of service users for whom the care home is proposed to be used, and the number of such users by reference to –

(a)   their sex;

(b)   the categories listed in paragraph 6(c) of Schedule 7;

(c)   service users who are children.

Index

Index of Cases

General

Islington LBC ex p. Rixon 1996 8

R on the Application of Bodimeade and others v Camden LBC 2001 113

R on the Application of the Personal Representatives of Christopher Beeson v Dorset Council 2001 115

R on the Application of Daly and Home Secretary 2001 128

R on the Application of Westminster CC v NASS 2001 80

R v Avon CC ex p. M 1999 82

R v Hammersmith and Fulham LBC ex p. M 1997 78

R v Islington LBC ex p. Batantu 2000 80

R v Leicestershire CC ex p. Thompson 2000 128

R v Local Authority and Police Authority in the Midlands, ex p. L.M. 2000 113

R v Newham LBC ex p. Medical Foundation 1997 82, 89

R v Newham LBC ex p. P 2000 82

R v North Derbyshire Health Authority ex p. Fisher 1998 7

R v North and East Devon Health Authority ex p. Coughlan 1999 113

R v Richmond LBC ex p. P.T. 2000 82

R v Secretary of State for Education and Science v Tameside Metropolitan Borough Council 1977 128

R v Sefton MBC ex p. Help The Aged 1997 79, 81

R v South Lanarkshire Council ex p. McGregor 2001 81

R v Sutton LBC ex p. Turner 1998 8

R v Wandsworth LBC ex p. O 2000 79

R v Wigan MBC ex p. Tammadge 1998

Re F 2000 32

Shah v Barnet LBC 1983 77

Human Rights Act

Abdulaziz, Cabales and Balkandali v UK 1985 115

Acmanne v Belgium 1993 112

Airey v Ireland 1979 112

Association X v UK 1975 107

Botta v Italy 1998 110–111

C v UK 1983 114

Chassagnou v France 1999 109

Costello-Roberts v UK 1993 110

D v UK 1997 108

D.S. and E.S. v UK 1990 114

Dubowska and Skup v Poland 1997 114

Dudgeon v UK 1981 110

Edwards v UK 2001 115

Gaskin v UK 1989 113

Guerra v Italy 1998 112

Halford v UK 1997 112

Handyside v UK 1976 109

Herczegafalvy v Austria 1993 108

Ireland v UK 1976 108

Lopez-Ostra v Spain 1994 112

Marzari v Italy 1999 111–112

Niemitz v Germany 1992 110

Malone v UK 1996 115

Osman v UK 1999 107

Rees v UK 1986 110

Ribitsch v Austria 1992 108

Tanko v Finland 1994 108

Thlimmennos v Greece 2000 115

Tomasi v France 1992 108

X and Y v UK 1983 113

X and Y v Netherlands 1985 112

Z v Finland 1997 113

Public Interest Disclosure Act

Bladon v ALM Medical Services Ltd 1999 140

Boughton v National Tyre Ltd 2000 140

Chattenton v City of Sunderland City Council 1999 140

Fernandes v Netcom Consultants Ltd 2000 142

Stephens v Englishcombe House Residential Home 2000 140

Printed in the United Kingdom
by Lightning Source UK Ltd.
111702UKS00001B/97-126